THE BALD EAGLE

BALD EAGLE

JIM SMITH
and MARK DAWSON

MAINSTREAM
PUBLISHING

*To my wife, Yvonne, for putting up with me so much
over the years*

First published in Great Britain 1990 by
MAINSTREAM PUBLISHING COMPANY
(EDINBURGH) LTD
7 Albany Street
Edinburgh EH1 3UG
ISBN 1 85158 382 3 (cloth)

British Library Cataloguing in Publication Data

Smith, Jim
  1. England. Association football. Clubs. Management.
  Smith, Jim
  I. Title   II. Dawson, Mark
  328.76179633463092

  ISBN 1-85158-382-3

Typeset in 11pt on 13pt Imprint by Blackpool Typesetting
  Services Ltd
Printed in Great Britain by Billings & Sons Ltd, Worcester

CONTENTS

Chapter 1

BEGINNINGS

FIGHTING FIT

FOOTBALLERS have used many weird and wonderful training methods, but not many can say they had to put on boxing gloves and get thumped to boost their careers. Yet that is what I did as a schoolkid trying to make my mark in the game.

My first contact with organised soccer was at Firth Park Grammar School in Sheffield where I captained the school team. But there was one major problem – there was no proper football training. Even in those days fitness was very important to me and that's how I came to be a boxing champion. The school's boxing club, run by a Mr Pengelly, offered regular training sessions and so I joined up. I only wanted to get fit for soccer by doing weight training and gym work, but there was a catch. If you joined the boxing club you had to box.

I know football can be a hard game but, believe me, boxing is a lot harder and, to be honest, I never really liked it. But I must have had some talent because I became Sheffield champion and a beaten finalist for the Yorkshire title.

I started throwing punches as a 12-year-old and my second bout was an inter-house contest. I hit the lad and he started to cry, so I stopped, but everyone was shouting 'Go on, hit him again!' I obliged and he started crying again, but thankfully they stopped the fight there.

My success took me to the final of the Sheffield championship and a date with a young lad called Johnny Fitzpatrick. He was from a big boxing family – his brother was a professional and he was heading for the pro game himself. I remember that every time I hit him he just smiled at me. Then he started hitting me on the nose and I was not smiling back. I lost the fight and my good looks!

In my second bid for the title I won it and was dead chuffed. But there was a drawback . . . I now had to go to Leeds for the county championships. As I was being gloved up for the quarter-final bout, I asked the second about my opponent. 'Oh, this lad loves fighting, he thrives on it – he's from the remand home,' said my helpful second. I just wanted to know why they had let him out.

Still, I won that scrap and then had a real humdinger in the semi-final. I was well bashed up, but managed to win again. I lost a close points decision in the Yorkshire final, but I did get to meet one of my idols, the former British heavyweight champ Bruce Woodstock who was presenting the prize.

It would have been nice to have been the Yorkshire champion, but if I had won I would just have had to fight some bugger else in the national championships and the opponents were getting bigger. At least it made up my mind that boxing was not going to be my career – it was too hard for me – so I decided to concentrate on football, where a knowledge of the pugilistic art can be a distinct advantage.

I don't know where my interest in the game came from as there was no sporting background in the family. The only sport my dad, Jim, liked was horse racing and that was because he did a bit of bookmaking at Doncaster and other local courses in his spare time.

We lived on the Shiregreen council estate in Sheffield – dad, my mum, Doris, and my three sisters, Doreen, Jean and my twin, Barbara. My father, who died when I was 21, was a wheelwright by trade. When that profession petered out, he started his own business – a bodyworks for lorries – which he ran for 20 years. I always remember one piece of advice from my dad – 'Jim, for heaven's sake get your feet going, because your hands are useless.' My first school was Hartley Brook Junior & Infants, but they did not play football there. Rounders was the game and I did not fare badly at that. But in my spare

Jim Smith (front row, centre) *captain of Firth Park Grammar School football team*

Jim Smith (front row, centre) *captain of Firth Park Grammar School cricket team*

time I was playing soccer in the schoolyard and in the street. I suppose I just did it because all the other kids did it too.

Sport soon dominated my school life, with football in winter and cricket in summer, and it had a detrimental effect on my academic development. I had the ability to do better, but I never studied hard enough and I left school at 16 with one 'O' level, in history. The only thing I remember about it now is Vasco Da Gama – and they are a football team, anyway!

My history teacher was 'Spike' Johnson, who also ran the football team. He said I would never make it as a professional footballer and my mum said I would never get an 'O' level, so I proved them both wrong. I still keep in contact with 'Spike' – he is in his 80s now – and met up with him again when Newcastle played Sheffield United.

While at Firth Park, I joined a team called New Cross United in the next estate to Shiregreen. A pal of mine, Keith Phillips, introduced me to them and we used to make the three-mile walk every Thursday night for the team meeting when we would pay our shilling subscription. The Grammar School only played friendlies so as a 14-year-old I got my first taste of competitive soccer with New Cross. I was playing Saturday mornings for the school and afternoons in the Sheffield Under-16 League.

In my second year with New Cross, we were drawn against Sheffield United's nursery team, Oaksfold, in a Cup semi-final. We lost 3–2, but Reg Wright, who was on the staff at United, asked me to go along for a trial. The trial match was with the Under-18 Northern Intermediate League side away to Leeds United and we were to meet at Bramall Lane. But when I got there, I was so nervous I just stood outside the dressing-room biting my nails away. Luckily, Reg Wright came out to buy the team's sandwiches from the shop across the road and walked straight into me, otherwise my career might never have got underway.

We played on the main pitch at Elland Road, which was brilliant for all the lads, and won 2–1. I was three years younger than some of the players, but I played up front and scored. That was when I first met the late Joe Mercer, the Sheffield United manager, who watched the game from the touchline with Leeds manager Don Revie. Joe came into our dressing-room at half-time, shook my hand and said: 'Look, you've tied your socks up wrong.' And he undid my socks and showed me how to tie them up properly.

I was invited to join United and the following season I was playing for Oaksfold, who were run by Lol Swallow, a famous name in the Sheffield area. I was a forward in those days and scored goals by the hatful – 123 in one season, including ten in one semi-final. But my problem was that I was not quick enough at the higher level and I moved back to midfield. Someone once wrote that I would have played for England if I had had pace. They may have been being generous to my talents, but they pinpointed the problem.

Every player at Oaksfold was in his school's representative side – Sheffield, Rotherham, Chesterfield, Denaby etc – except me. Our headmaster reckoned the kids took too much time off to play for the town and he put the block on it. Still, I was not complaining – I got an occasional game with the Northern Intermediate team and I trained twice a week at Bramall Lane.

Funnily enough, Sheffield Wednesday had always been my team as a kid. Though the first League game I ever went to watch was Sheffield United v Nottingham Forest, I and all my pals were Wednesday-ites. There was a great rivalry between the two clubs, but it was sporting and good-natured. Sadly, that sort of rivalry seems to have died out in modern times. Now things get much more intense and that brings out an evil side which blights the game.

One of my biggest regrets is that I never played for Wednesday – and I never even got to play at Hillsborough. Another big regret is that when I left school I did not join United's ground staff but instead decided to look to a career outside the game. I am not saying I would have made the grade at Bramall Lane, but I would have had a hell of a better chance as a ground staff boy.

Really, I was caught between two stools – was I going to make it as a footballer, or should I look to my future and try and follow a profession? In the end, I joined Tinsley Wire Industries as a trainee manager, which involved spending a few months in each department. So, instead of being at the club every day, I was only part-time with United and I know that cost me in my soccer career.

Nevertheless, I was made captain of the Northern Intermediates and, in 1958, went for an England Youth trial at Corby. I was picked as right-half for the Possibles, while a young Nobby Stiles had the same position for the Probables. I don't remember Nobby kicking me, but I do recall that he had all his teeth in those days. Geoff Hurst was also in the trial, as was Charlie Mitten's son, John, who went on to play for Newcastle, Leicester and Coventry.

After 20 minutes, snow started to fall like you have never seen and the game was abandoned. We were to be informed of the England team the following week, but in the meantime I was persuaded to sign as a part-time professional by United's chief scout Archie Clark. Joe Mercer had just left Sheffield to take over at Aston Villa and I think they were keen to get me signed up in case Joe came in for me. It seemed like a good move as I was put on a wage of £9 per week – not bad in those days – but it robbed me of an England Youth cap. England would not pick professionals for the youth team and most of the other lads were ground staff boys who, though they were being paid by their clubs, were not classed as pros. As a part-time

Jim Smith and Willie Carlin at an Under-18 England coaching session at Lilleshall

Joe Mercer . . . my first manager at Sheffield United

professional, I was no longer eligible for England. That was a shame because everyone called up for the trial eventually got a game – they would pick up their one cap, say 'Thank you very much' and then sign professional.

At Tinsley Wire Industries, I was moved to the stores department which meant Saturday working. I offered to do an extra hour every weekday to get Saturdays off, but they would not agree so I quit and worked for my dad before moving on to a fish market.

John Harris replaced Joe Mercer at the club and while Joe had been ready to give the kids a chance, Harris went back to the senior players. Sheffield United were a big club, yo-yoing between the First and Second Divisions. They had over 30 pros – players like Alan Hodgkinson, Joe Shaw, Graham Shaw, Ceo Coldwell, Gerry Summers, Willie Hamilton and 'Doc' Pace – and when you were just a part-timer, you were always going to be struggling to get a break. So, at the age of 20 and still working in Baldock's fish market, I was given a free transfer without ever getting a game in the first team.

It was a tough time for me – I was about to get married and I was out of a job. Archie Clark recommended me to Dave Smith at Aldershot and I became a full-time footballer at last.

I don't know if there were signing-on fees in those days, but I didn't get one. However, I did get £13 per week in the summer; £17 in winter; and £20 when in the first team. And so I duly made my Football League début in a Fourth Division clash at a lovely place called Workington. As best I remember, we drew and I had a decent match.

The next game was at top-of-the-table Bradford City when a big gate of 8,000 saw the home team win. At the end of the match there was a knock on our dressing-room door and there stood my father. I do not know how he had got past the stewards, but I was totally embarrassed and quickly ushered him out. He had hardly ever been to watch me play before, but then this was the big time!

One of the best moments of my time at Aldershot was when we reached the third round of the FA Cup and were drawn against First Division Aston Villa, whose star striker was Tony Hateley. We held them 0–0 at Villa Park before beating them 3–1 in the replay in front of 16,000 fans. Joe Mercer was managing Villa and he had a chat with me afterwards. I had brief dreams of him signing me for Villa, but it never happened.

While Dave Smith was the manager at Aldershot, Jimmy Sirrel, who went on to boss Brentford, Notts County and Sheffield United, was the guy who ran the show. He acted as coach, physio, scout and groundsman, and even decorated the dressing-rooms. What a character Jimmy was. My wife Yvonne and I had just had our first child, Alison, and I used to wheel her pram up to the ground on an afternoon just to hear Jimmy's tales of his days at Celtic.

He claimed to be the best uncapped winger in Scottish football, though people who played with him told me he could have hurdled for Scotland, too!

He moved from Celtic to join Bradford City and said that was when he really knew he was in football, when someone spat at him for the first time in a match.

Jimmy influenced me greatly in terms of his coaching, his great enthusiasm and his belief in smartness. Aldershot was only a little club, but the kit and training gear were always spotless and the dressing-rooms and physio's room were always clean.

We once had to rope Jimmy into our annual pre-season cricket match against a local club side, even though he had never played the game in his life before. They batted first and Jimmy had a nightmare with the ball going through his legs and catches being dropped. We were left to chase over 200 runs to win. As our innings got underway, Jimmy headed for the nets holding a bat for the first time and spent an hour practising. He was called into action at 60-6, which was desperation stakes as the game was in danger of finishing before the pub opened. Hitting the ball to square leg, he ran one and then went for an impossible second. The ball was returned to the wicket-keeper with Jimmy only halfway down the wicket but – to let him stay in a bit longer – the keeper deliberately missed the stumps. Jimmy snapped: 'You're not making an idiot of me – I'm out!' and off he walked. Somehow that sums up the man.

I enjoyed my four years at Aldershot, though we never got out of the Fourth Division, but at the age of 24 I found myself on another free transfer.

The problem was that I was due a benefit the next season which guaranteed me an automatic £500 from the club. And you are on dangerous ground when a hard-up outfit like Aldershot knows it will have to stump up £500.

So I moved on to Halifax Town under Willie Watson, who was one of my heroes because he had played cricket for

Yorkshire and England. A lovely fellow, he had represented his country at both soccer and cricket, but the summer game was his real passion. I was team skipper and I would go to his office to discuss football matters to find he only wanted to talk cricket.

Willie's dream was always to run a cricket team in the summer and a football team in the winter – and that is exactly what he finally achieved when he moved to South Africa.

Before that, however, Willie left Halifax to manage Bradford City and Vic Metcalfe took over, only to be replaced shortly afterwards by Alan Ball Senior. Not only was I the Halifax captain, I had not missed a game in two years until Alan Ball arrived. He dropped me after two games and I never got back in.

Ball had a very abrasive style of management that was based on fear and I am sure that was what was behind him dropping me. He thought he would leave out the one bloke no one expected him to drop – that was his frightener theory and it established his authority. As a manager now, I realise that it is very important to establish yourself with a new group of players. But I would rather do it by demanding higher standards than by Ball's method. On the plus side, he had some very good coaching ideas and his fitness training was unbelievably intense – the hardest I have ever had – and it often meant coming back in the afternoon for a second session.

While Ball started out with this amazing intensity, it gradually tailed off and he started missing training. He would arrive at lunchtime and say we were not working hard enough and make us report back in the afternoon to suit his timetable. Often, he left the training to Harry Hubbick, another remarkable character. Ball was also involved in his son's garage and would spend his time selling cars on the side while we were waiting for a team meeting. As skipper, I had to get him out of the office where he was on the phone flogging a motor.

I always had the feeling with Alan Ball that he thought he should be managing somewhere better than Halifax; that he was too good for the club.

His right-hand man, Harry Hubbick, was something else. He had played for Bolton Wanderers when they *were* Bolton Wanderers and they say Stanley Mathews never got a kick

16

Willie Watson . . . my boss at Halifax Town

against him – or, at least, Stanley got a few kicks, but they weren't of the ball.

Harry was not the brightest of men – at training he would say: 'Fifty per cent go with him; fifty per cent go with him; and the other fifty per cent come with me.'

When Ball started missing training, we would tell Harry to go easy on us. He would say: 'OK, but when you go past the manager's office, breathe heavy!'

Harry would have us doing sprints and would shout: 'On your marks . . . go!' but would forget which hand he had the whistle in and stick his finger in his mouth and blow.

I remember him once driving from the training ground to Halifax's Shay stadium with a few of the lads in his car. He had to turn right to enter the ground, but did not indicate and an overtaking car smashed into the side of him. A furious Harry got out and bellowed at the driver: 'You daft bugger, you could see I was turning into the ground, I've got my track suit on!'

On another occasion we had a mock tribunal for Tony Field, who had been sent off, and the verdict was a £25 fine and 28 days. 'Wait a minute,' said Harry, 'Shouldn't we give him a £25 fine and a month!' And he was serious.

There were certainly a few laughs at Halifax – and some of the football was not bad either. One year we drew Bishop Auckland in the FA Cup. No one knew much about them except that they were famous for getting to Wembley an amazing number of times in the Amateur Cup. We assumed they would have a nice ground and a good stadium, but it can best be described as a tip. The pitch had a lot of snow and ice and the game should never have been played, but we scrambled a lucky 0–0 draw. In the dressing-room, which was like an old barnhouse, this big bloke was talking to the Auckland players.

'We are all right now, boys,' he said. 'We'll beat them down there. It is a better pitch which will suit our football.'

The big fella turned out to be Lawrie McMenemy and we beat them 6–0 in the replay. I have mentioned that game to Lawrie a few times over the years, but he does not seem to recollect it!

Even though we hammered the Bishops, they insisted on taking the mickey out of our lads.

Alan Ball Senior . . . abrasive manager at Halifax Town

Lawrie McMenemy . . . boss at Bishop Auckland

'You lot will never get to Wembley,' they said, 'but we will be there in the Amateur Cup.'

The following week they played Skelmersdale in the Amateur Cup and lost!

After Alan Ball brought my ever-present record to an abrupt halt, I asked him to let me go, but he said no and that he would be offering me a new two-year contract. The next day he sold me to Lincoln City.

Still, at least I was no longer a free-transfer man. I changed hands for the princely sum of £500. Lincoln manager Ron Gray always said he played a game of snooker for me with Ball. It was one price if Ron won and a bit less if Bally won – I am still not sure of the result!

In action for Lincoln City against Brentford

Chapter 2

THE MOVE INTO MANAGEMENT

TOO OLD AT TWENTY-EIGHT

THERE MUST have come a point in my career when I had to accept that I was not the greatest right-half who ever pulled on a pair of boots . . . and a point soon after when I realised I was not even the best right-half to play in the Fourth Division. My enthusiasm and fitness were never in question, but it seemed I lacked that special something to give me a shot at the big-time. And so I slogged around Division Four – setting for all my 247 League games – with the likes of Aldershot, Halifax and Lincoln City. And yet I can honestly say I loved it. Glamour and money were thin on the ground, but there were the characters, the laughs and the pleasure of playing the game.

I was 27 when I arrived at Lincoln – a lovely little ground in an attractive city. But there was one problem, the team was holding up the rest of the League and it had had to seek re-election for the past four years. And yet joining Lincoln was probably the best move I ever made . . . it got me close to Boston and the crucial switch to management that, though I did not know it, was just around the corner.

The move also saw me buy my first house, with my signing-on fee supplying the deposit. I had always lived in club houses up until then, but Yvonne and I now had three girls – Alison, Suzanne and Fiona – and we needed a place of our own.

We lost the first two games after my arrival and the

re-election bid was already being prepared. But then we had a fabulous run and finished halfway up the table.

Graham Taylor was added to the squad the next season, 1968–69, and we suddenly found ourselves going for promotion. We also made the third round of the FA Cup where we lost 2–1 to Birmingham City, with yours truly scoring. But then manager Ron Gray made what I considered a vital mistake. He sold our six-foot three gangling giraffe of a striker Norman Corner to Bradford City and bought Alick Jeffrey to replace him. An England Under-23 international, Alick had been a prolific scorer with Doncaster Rovers. He was a great bloke for playing cards and having a sing-song on the coach, but his best days were gone.

In the end, the club had its best season for years, but was just pipped for promotion by Bradford. Things could all have been so much different if we had gone up, but instead I found myself in a familiar position – available on a free transfer.

Watched by Jim Smith, Ray Harford heads clear for Lincoln v. Doncaster Rovers

There was always that worry coming to the end of a season when your fate would arrive sealed in an envelope. If you got a registered envelope, it was to tell you that you were being retained; if you got a brown envelope, it was a free. In fact, Ron Gray told me to my face that I was on my way. The explanation was that the directors thought I was too old at 28! I was choked – I had done a very good job for them.

Word got out quickly, because that afternoon I got a phone call from Ron Ashman, the manager of Scunthorpe, offering to take me there. Curiously enough, Lincoln had one game left the following weekend – the Lincolnshire Cup final against Scunthorpe. At the same time, the reserves had a match at Chesterfield. As I was getting a free transfer, I obviously would not be in the first team and I did not fancy the trip with the reserves. It is the only time that I have refused to play, but I went to Gray and said I would not turn out for the second string as I would not do myself justice. I was amazed when Ron said: 'Sod the directors, you're back in the first team.'

The night before the Cup final, the local evening paper had its back page and two inside pages full of letters from angry fans slamming the club for freeing me. 'What the hell is the club doing getting rid of Jim Smith?' it said, and I must admit it felt very gratifying. The furore spilled over into the Scunthorpe match as I took to the field with the fans chanting my name, and the support for me continued throughout the 90 minutes. In the dressing-room afterwards one of the younger directors came up to me and said: 'You're not leaving!'

We always went for a drink after the match to a pub called The Centurion, and in there Ron Gray and one of the directors asked to see me on the Monday when they would have a new contract for me. I went along to see them, knowing that I had a job at Scunthorpe up my sleeve and that gave me a little bargaining power.

In those days there was a statutory £250 signing-on fee and so I asked for that, but they refused to pay out and we were deadlocked. Realising I was getting nowhere, I arranged to see Ron Ashman. I had never had a decent signing-on fee in my life – nor made much money – and with a growing family and my career no longer in its first flush of youth, I was looking for a good deal. I asked Ashman for the £250, but he proceeded to explain Scunthorpe's wonderful bonus-points system which meant you picked up extra money for length of service. It looked to me as if I would need to be there ten years to get any decent cash.

I had gone to Scunthorpe with Yvonne and we decided to have a look round the place. We asked a bloke where the town centre was and he said: 'You're in it!' No, I did not fancy Scunthorpe too much.

Back home I went to see my mate Peter Kearns, who was four years older than me and had also just got a free from Lincoln. There was a big Mercedes outside his house and I went in wondering who it belonged to. Inside, Pete was talking to Ernest Malkinson, the chairman of Boston United. Malkinson was trying to sign Pete up and he asked me to join Boston, too. I said: 'I believe you have just sacked your manager. I'll consider coming as player-manager.'

I had been giving some thought to a career after my playing days were over and the possibility of management had crossed my mind. Now, here was a golden opportunity to get a foot in the door. Boston United had one game left and I went along to watch them. I just had a positive gut-feeling about the job and I suddenly knew I really wanted it. There were other appealing factors apart from the chance to get into management. Ernest Malkinson put a few pound notes on to the table, which had never happened to me before.

I finally plucked up the courage to ring Ron Ashman and tell him I was joining Boston in the Northern Premier League. He had already heard and said I would regret it – he had been a player-manager at Norwich and reckoned it was too difficult to handle both roles.

Funnily enough, the following season – after we had put Lincoln out – Boston United went to Scunthorpe in the Lincolnshire Cup and won 5–2. 'I wish I had given you that £250,' Ashman told me.

That summer of 1969, I was a manager at 28 and starting a career which has given me more satisfaction than my playing days. I was also earning more money than I had ever got before – and this was non-League football.

Boston only had one player on their books when I arrived and that worked very well for me. It meant I could bring in all my own players, though it also meant an incredibly hectic period. I signed a lot of experienced League players as part-timers and we had to do our pre-season training at Lincoln and Newark as none of the squad lived within 60 miles of Boston.

My first game in charge was against Great Harwood, who boasted England internationals Ronnie Clayton and Bryan Douglas, as well as Welsh star Roy Vernon. It was worrying seeing names of that calibre on the team sheet, but we won 4–0. Coincidentally, Great Harwood, who had strong connections with Blackburn Rovers, had a chairman called Derek Keighley who was later instrumental in my becoming manager of Blackburn.

Those early days at Boston were a remarkable time for me. I was virtually running a one-man show which meant long hours and a lot of hard work, but it was also great fun and a tremendous learning experience. As well as being full-time manager, I was the club secretary and, at the end of my first season there, I concreted the car park, dug the drains for the pitch and decorated the boardroom. I went back 12 years later and it was my wallpaper still hanging there, so I must have done a good job! When we lost our commercial manager, I had to run the club lottery. And when we reached the third round of the FA Cup – a brilliant achievement – and played Portsmouth at home in an all-ticket game, I spent the Friday night sticking the numbers on the wooden benches to signify the seats we had sold. It was, quite simply, the most hectic period of my life, but I did have some help. Yvonne volunteered to do the wages – even mine, though she stopped short of deducting her housekeeping at source. And she and the trainer's wife opened a little tea bar which they ran in a corner of the ground.

As well as running the club, there was also the little matter of managing the team. One of my first moves was to insist that they wore collars and ties on match days. The lads were part-timers and some used to come to a game straight from work and still wearing their overalls. I was not having that. I had picked up the notion of smartness and a professional image from the

Bobby Svarc . . . with me at Boston United and Colchester

likes of Jimmy Sirrel and I was gradually bringing in other bits and pieces that I had picked up from my own bosses.

But I suppose, at the end of the day, the biggest lesson I had learnt from all my clubs was to play good football. All my managers, from Joe Mercer onwards, wanted to do that and the lesson had stood me in good stead – play football, as opposed to kick-and-rush, and you will get results in the end.

The players accepted my demands happily. I was still playing and would have a drink and a laugh with them, but I could also distance myself when needed. Discipline was not a problem and I think that was because they respected me as a player – I could still do it on the pitch. Plus, they were on very good money to stay on it. A lot of the lads from League soccer wished they had gone non-League sooner because it was better financially.

I was fortunate to be at Boston during a great period for non-League football – an era of tremendous quality. There were people like Gordon Milne who had come out of League management to take over at Wigan Athletic, and Peter Swales, who was chairman of Altrincham before going on to take the reins at Manchester City. It was very competitive and a good grounding for a young manager because non-League chairmen still demand success for their money. I suppose it was a little like going to university.

I always tried to balance the books and I learnt the contractual side of the game. I had only been involved in contract negotiations from a player's side before – and I had hardly been a roaring success at it – but now I got the other view. Handling players' contracts was hard for me then and I still find it hard even today. If the toughest job for a manager is to tell a young kid that he is not going to make the grade, the next toughest is to negotiate a deal with a player. And, of course, it is getting more difficult and more complicated. Now you sit round a table with agents, accountants and solicitors who all want their pound of flesh.

Though I never managed to win the Northern Premier League at Boston, we enjoyed much success and, on one occasion, applied for the League. But, as was the case in those days, the Division Four clubs clung together and all those seeking re-election got it. I would have loved the present set-up where the GM Vauxhall Conference offers direct promotion to Division Four. We knocked League clubs out of the FA Cup and, in terms of ability, we were good enough for the League.

I had three years as player-manager at Boston and it had not taken long for me to decide that management was for me. But while I loved the club, I knew that if I wanted a real crack at my new profession I had to get back into the Football League.

The number two job to Lawrie McMenemy at Grimsby Town had been offered to me and I had had an interview with

Jim Smith and Boston United chairman Ernest Malkinson

Lawrie, but it had not felt right. Grimsby were in the basement and at that level you don't really have assistant managers . . . you have someone to run on with the sponge for the first team and then take the reserves midweek. However, Lawrie won promotion with Grimsby and 18 months later was leading Southampton out in the FA Cup final at Wembley. I wonder if I did the right thing turning him down – I might have been at Wembley with him.

Anyway, having resolved that my future lay in League management, I applied for the vacancy at Colchester United in November 1972. It is the only manager's job I have ever applied for and it is possibly only down to a little bit of cheek that I landed it.

I went along to watch Colchester play at Peterborough and meet the chairman, Roy Chapman. Colchester were in a position I knew well – bottom of the Fourth Division – but they got a draw and Mr Chapman and his fellow directors seemed very pleased at what they judged a good result. I told them their team was a load of rubbish – 'Boston United would have beaten both teams out there tonight.' It was a touch of arrogance, but it helped make me a Football League manager just a few weeks after my 32nd birthday.

There was a year left on my contract with Boston, but Ernest Malkinson typically wished me well and let me move straight on to Colchester, telling me to come back if things did not work out.

I have to admit I was nervous taking over the reins at Colchester. The team were in a lot of trouble – bottom of the table and with a poor side – and I had to prove that I had what it takes to run a League club. The previous boss, Dick Graham, had left through ill-health . . . it was that kind of job.

My first game in charge was against Mansfield, who were going for promotion, and we drew 1–1 which was a satisfactory start. Things got better, for we had an FA Cup success over Bournemouth, who were flying high under John Bond, and I won the divisional Manager of the Month award in my first month. Sadly, it did not last and Colchester had to apply for re-election at the end of the season. Fortunately, the other clubs took pity and voted us in. It had been a tough baptism for me,

The family moves to Colchester
(left to right) *Fiona, wife Yvonne, Alison and Suzanne*

but my enthusiasm was undimmed and, in fact, I had found it easier to adapt than I had feared.

Joe Hooley had joined us as coach. He had a lot of ability, but could not handle the pressure of winning and losing and he quit. My next coaching appointment was ex-Leicester player Bobby Roberts from Coventry who had impressed me at Lilleshall, and he did a great job. United were so bad that both Bobby and myself had to turn out for the team during that first season. In fact, I would say Bobby was our best player!

It was while at Colchester that I met Bobby Robson, who was boss at Ipswich then. I even did a deal with him once to take striker Micky Hill on loan. Micky had been giving Ipswich problems by refusing to turn up for training and we suffered the same problems – no sign of Micky. Eventually, I went round to his house and found it strewn with newspapers and inhabited by a duck and its ducklings, which Hill had taken from a pond in the local park. He was a strange bloke. He promised to come to training, but only bothered to turn up a couple of times, so we had to knock it on the head.

But I did do some worthwhile deals, including signing two players I had taken to Boston – John Froggatt and Bobby Svaro, a very good goalscorer. At £1,500 from Lincoln, Svaro had been Boston's biggest signing, while Froggatt had cost £500 from Buxton. I took them both to Colchester for £6,000 which represented good business for my old club, and I also bought Ray Harford and 'keeper Mickey Walker. The changes did the trick because next season we were promoted and the following year held our own in Division Three.

Not everything worked out smoothly at Colchester. I could have signed Brian Talbot, who was languishing in Ipswich reserves, but we could not stump up the £12,000. And John Gregory was available at Northampton for £9,000, but again we did not have the cash.

My achievements at Colchester got me noticed by Blackburn Rovers, where Derek Keighley, who knew me from non-League days as chairman of Great Harwood, was by now a director. I had had a tentative approach from Blackburn early on in my time at Colchester, but they had decided I was not experienced enough and the job had gone to Gordon Lee. Gordon had taken them to Division Two and was very highly regarded. But now he was quitting Rovers to take control at Newcastle United and I was approached again and appointed in 1975.

It was an unusual situation because a new man often comes in when a team is struggling, but here was I stepping into a successful set-up. When a team is on the skids, the players are desperate for an up-turn and respond more readily to a new voice. At Blackburn, I faced resentment from a bunch of players worried that I was going to break up their winning formula. They were always moaning that 'Gordon would have done this . . .' or 'Gordon would have done that . . .' But there was a tremendous team spirit and some good players at the club and I had to allay their fears that I was there to split up the team.

I had a different style to Gordon Lee and I changed some of the training methods, but the few changes I made to the team were very gradual. I converted John Bailey from a left-winger

David Wagstaffe . . . deadline signing for Blackburn from Wolves

to a left-back and Kevin Hird from right-wing to right-back and in deadline week, when we were in a spot of trouble, I snapped up Dave Wagstaffe, from Wolves, and Gordon Taylor, from Birmingham, for £3,000 each. Those two signings helped keep us in the Second Division. Waggy had great talent and proved an especially inspired buy – even though he was so nervous that we had to push him out on to the pitch and he would have a cigarette lit up within seconds of coming off.

Noel Brotherston was another good signing for Blackburn. I remembered him playing for Tottenham reserves at Colchester and I moved in when Spurs freed him.

A very strong team developed at Rovers, with players like Paul Bradshaw, Stuart Metcalfe, Derek Fazakerley, Tony Parkes and Graham Hawkins. But I was never given the money to get the striker I needed to make it a promotion team. I tried bringing John Byron back to the club and I also bought former England and Arsenal star John Radford from West Ham, but they did not provide the answer up front.

The player I really wanted was Steve Kindon and I knew I could do a deal with Wolves for £70,000. It was a fair price for an England Youth international and proven scorer, but the directors could not come up with the money. Kindon signed for our big rivals, Burnley, who were struggling at the bottom of the Second Division, and his goals helped keep them up. That was fine for Burnley, but as far as I was concerned, his goals could have put us into the First Division. It was a frustrating situation and it showed that my ambitions would be limited with Blackburn.

Perhaps it was just as well that a new opportunity was just around the corner.

Steve Kindon . . . the striker I needed for Blackburn Rovers

Chapter 3

RELEGATED AND SACKED

£1 MILLION I DID NOT WANT TO SPEND

I AM very much a man of instinct when it comes to football
. . . and especially where clubs are concerned. When a job comes
along – and I have had more than my fair share of offers – I
usually get a gut feeling about it and, more often than not, that
feeling is what will decide the issue.

When I was at Blackburn, I was offered the manager's post
at West Bromwich Albion and one of my biggest mistakes was
that I did not take it. I just did not get the right vibes; it did
not feel right. But West Brom is a good club and I am sure I
could have done well at The Hawthorns. Ron Atkinson was
next on their list and he snapped up the offer and made a success
of it. I did not know Ron then, though he was to become a big
mate, but I had played against him and he had come from the
same non-League background as myself.

I was feeling a bit disillusioned with Blackburn and the lack
of money available to round off my team-building when there
was an approach from Birmingham City. This time, the guts
said 'Go for it!' The prospect excited me – even though it was
to lead to my first ever relegation as a boss, and the sack!

Just before I moved to St Andrews I got a phone call from
Lawrie McMenemy asking me to meet him at an England
Under–21 game in Manchester. He said he had some informa-
tion for me and I thought: 'Lawrie's going to Birmingham and
he's going to ask me to take over at Southampton.' It shows how

wrong you can be when it comes to the managerial merry-go-round. Shortly before I left for Manchester I got a call from an Adidas marketing manager who told me that the Birmingham job was mine for the asking and when I met Lawrie it turned out he was trying to fix me up with Plymouth Argyle. So it was St Andrews for me and a team bottom of the First Division with just 16 games to go in the 1977–78 season.

Birmingham had sacked the former Leeds United full-back Willie Bell and had brought in Sir Alf Ramsey, with the title of consultant director, to take the reins during the interim. It could have been strange following a legend like Sir Alf and it could also have been very instructive if he had been allowed to stay and help me. He had a great football brain and his 1966 World Cup-winning team was one of the best teams I have ever seen. I am not sure what sort of a combination we would have made, but the idea of me as team manager with Alf advising appealed to me greatly. I know I could have benefited from his experience. However, it did not happen because of Ramsey's feud with the Birmingham chairman Keith Coombs. While Ramsey knew he was only keeping the seat warm, he would have loved to have stayed on as an advisor. But not only was he moved over to make way for me, he was moved right out of the club. The Ramsey v Coombs situation was so strained that he had to go – and with bad feeling on both sides.

I met Alf later at a football writers' dinner, but it was not a very inspiring chat. All he did was knock Birmingham City and the chairman. Ramsey felt bitter about it, but then he felt bitter about a lot of things.

So it was up to me to save City from the drop and, with a little help from a young superstar called Trevor Francis, that is exactly what I did.

But I feared the worst when I walked into the place. A player called Archie Styles was on the treatment table and his first words to his new boss were: 'Do we still get our bonus when we are out injured?' I had no doubts where his priorities lay and he did not stay at the club long enough to find out the answer to his question.

City had players like Jim Montgomery, Paddy Howard, Joe Gallagher, Gary Pendrey, Malcolm Page, Tony Towers,

Terry Hibbitt, Keith Bertschin and John Connolly, but Francis was the key man. We were in a corner and, as I usually do in that sort of situation, I went for experience, dropping a couple of the kids, Kevin Dillon and Kevin Broadhurst.

Don't get me wrong, I love to have young players in the team, but you find that the older players can handle the pressure a lot better.

The mood was very down at St Andrews – there was no life and no interest about the place. I planned to watch the first game – against Newcastle United in midweek – before saying anything, but things were so bad that I blew my top straight away. And I carried on in that vein after the Newcastle match. We had been leading 1–0 but conceded a late equaliser through someone not doing their job. I stormed into the dressing-room and shouted: 'That's useless!', plus a few choice expletives, and smashed all the cups to the floor. But I knew what I was doing – they were plastic cups!

I seem to have acquired a bit of a reputation for losing my temper and hurling cups and saucers about the dressing-room, but I have to come clean and say that it is mostly exaggerated. I did chuck a few things around in my non-League days, but I have calmed down over the years. However, the odd outburst can still be effective and it worked at Birmingham. They were not used to that sort of approach – it was neither Willie Bell's nor Alf Ramsey's style – and they were a bit taken aback. But they seemed to quite admire it and they certainly responded – especially Trevor Francis, who had been a star at the club since he was 16 and had asked for a transfer just before my arrival.

While the media were speculating on whom we would sell him to, I spent my first week at the club trying to get him to sign a new contract. He agreed to wait and see how things went . . . and they went very well. Trevor notched up nine goals in the last 16 games and most of them either won the game or got us a point. With Bertschin also scoring well, we enjoyed a great run and finished the season halfway up the table.

There were two particularly memorable games in that run-in – against Wolves, when I was stitched up by the Press, and against Nottingham Forest, when we were brilliant.

Sir Alf Ramsey . . . we never got the chance to work together

Wolves were also in relegation trouble and some reporters had asked me if I would like their prolific striker John Richards in my team. I said: 'Yes, he's a good player . . .' and that was it. Before the game, it was all over the back pages that I was trying to buy Richards and, after we had won and he had missed a penalty, the Wolves directors accused me of tapping their star man via the newspapers. It taught me a lesson about how the media can set you up.

We played so well against Forest in the last match that they said we would win the Championship the following season. Instead, we went down! Our impressive run at the end of the season lulled me into a false sense of security. I thought we were good enough to hold our own in the top flight and I must hold up my hands and admit I got it wrong.

I did not have a lot of cash to play with in the close season, but I did not spend it as well as I should. Thinking Jim Montgomery could still do a job in goal, I bought a young 'keeper to bring on. Unfortunately, Monty had already gone over the hill. I also brought in Alan Ainscow, who did all right, and Don Givens and Stewart Barrowclough in a swap deal with Newcastle that saw Terry Hibbitt and John Connolly heading for the North-East.

At the end of the previous season, when we were safe from the drop, I had left Hibbitt out to give one of the young lads a chance. That game stopped Hibbitt playing a full 42–game season and he was not happy. He started moaning that he wanted away from Birmingham. Not to me, mind, but loud enough that I could hear him. I learnt that Newcastle boss Bill McGarry wanted him, so I happily packed Hibbitt and Connolly off to St James's Park and took Barrowclough, a player who never realised his full potential. Some time later, when he had been sacked by Newcastle, McGarry rang me up and asked: 'How did you get on with that so-and-so Barrowclough?' I replied: 'Well how did you get on with those two so-and-so's Hibbitt and Connolly?' I had only got one winger, while he had picked up a pair. And both his went on free transfers, while I sold mine to Bristol Rovers for £80,000.

The 1978–79 season was a bitterly disappointing one. Our strike force of Francis and Bertschin suffered with injuries and they only scored 14 goals between them. We lost a lot of games by the odd goal and their tally of the previous season would have been enough to save us. In addition, Francis had spent the summer playing in the United States and he came back with his mind set on a move.

The season City went down, Trevor Francis became Britain's

John Richards . . . I was accused of tapping the Wolves goal ace

first ever £1 million player when I sold him to Brian Clough at Nottingham Forest – though, as I will explain later, the price was actually £999,999. That gave me cash to develop the team but, to be honest, I did not want it. Most managers dream of being handed £1 million and being told to go and spend it, but I did not think it was right for us. We had the nucleus of a good young team with the likes of Dillon, Broadhurst, Pat van den

41

Hauwe, Mark Dennis and Joe Gallagher and I said to Keith Coombs that if we were patient we would get back into the First Division with a strong squad that would still be developing. Coombs would have none of it. 'You've got the money, go out and buy. I want to go straight back up to Division One', was his message.

So I brought in several experienced, quality players – Colin Todd (from Everton), Archie Gemmill (from Forest), Frank Worthington (from Bolton), and Jeff Wealands (from Hull). I also got Willie Johnston on loan from West Brom and young Alan Curbishley from West Ham. And so Coombs got his wish – the money was spent and, come May 1980, Birmingham City were back with the élite. But there was a price to pay – the club went from £500,000 in the black to £300,000 in the red and the average age of the side had rocketed.

I became only the fifth manager to take a team down and straight back up, but it was a narrow squeak. We went into our last game against Notts County needing to win or draw to pip Chelsea on goal average and we battled our way to a nerve-shredding 3–3 draw.

We developed into a very useful First Division outfit, with a nice blend of the old heads I had bought and the young 'uns, and in our first season back we finished halfway.

The following season I brought in a couple of Dutch players – Tony van Miero and Budde Brocken – and I genuinely felt we were close to a Championship-challenging side. We played some smashing football, but the results would not go for us. We could not win away from home and the disciplinary record was bad, with the likes of Mark Dennis and Kevin Dillon getting themselves sent off.

As well as suspensions and injuries, we had tough draws in the FA Cup and League Cup and went out of both early. And another very significant thing happened – Ron Saunders, who had led Aston Villa to the glory of the League Championship the year before, quit.

Though I did not realise it at the time, the writing was on the wall for me from the moment that Saunders walked out of Villa Park. There were people in the Birmingham boardroom who immediately saw him as the man to win them the title.

Ready to score a century . . . cricket, one of my great loves

I lived about half-a-mile away from Ron, but I never got to know him. While most of the other managers in Birmingham socialised, Saunders was a big family man and a very private person.

I had felt under pressure for my job when we were relegated, but Coombs had stood by me – after all, I had been his choice. But now the pressure was back on with a string of poor results – you did not need to be a bloodhound to smell trouble.

We went to West Ham for a vital game and I swapped the team around, putting in the kids and bringing in an on-loan 'keeper. We were 1–0 up with a few minutes to go when the ball came into our box. It seemed like ten pairs of hands went for it and the ref gave a penalty which left the result at 1-1. I had felt that I maybe needed a win there to keep my job. What I did not know was that Ron Saunders had already been lined up and the decision to sack me had been taken before the West Ham match. And that was the real sickener. They allowed me to go through another 90 minutes of agony with my neck on the line when it had already been chopped off. I still feel badly about that.

Keith Coombs was not at the game – he was due to go on a world cruise – but the other directors only said things like 'Bad luck' to me afterwards. On the Monday morning I was getting shaved when I got a call that the chairman wanted to see me at the ground at ten o'clock. I considered cutting my throat, but thought better of it!

I surmised that the meeting meant one of two things – the sack for me, or the chairman had become so disillusioned that he was quitting.

I arrived at the ground at the same time as Keith Coombs and when I saw his Rolls Royce pull up outside the boardroom, rather than the offices which are in a separate building, I knew I was for the bullet.

It is the only time I have been sacked in my career and it was a very difficult time – it was like a death in the family. The players, staff and Press came round to my house, but everything seemed strange . . . as though I was in a different world. I think I drank a bottle of brandy that day, but you would not have known it – I was still as sober as a judge.

With Prince Charles at St Andrews, Birmingham, where Charles landed his helicopter for a Royal tour of the West Midlands

I accept that my results had not been good enough, but we were close to being a very good side and I believe the board were too hasty in axing me. To be fair to Ron Saunders, he phoned me and said he would not take over until my money had been sorted out with City. This was done quickly and Ron stepped into the breach.

Saunders used to taunt me about the team's poor disciplinary record and insisted he would sort the trouble-makers out in five minutes. Eighteen months later he still had not done it!

In some ways, the sack at Birmingham was a blessing in disguise, for it enabled me to go to Oxford United where I had great success and where the pressure was not as intense. Within two days of being booted out of St Andrews, I had been contacted by Oxford and had an interview set up with United's chairman Robert Maxwell.

Moving down to Division Three and an unfashionable club provided a sharp contrast to what I had been used to. I thought to myself: 'What am I doing here?' but it turned out to be the start of the most satisfying period of my career.

The people of the city were not football people; the pitch was sloping, and the office resembled a prison cell. But I was out of work and needed a job, so who was I to be fussy? It took me six months to adjust to the place, but the saving grace was that we still had a chance of promotion and that kept things going.

We did not go up and that was probably a good thing. It gave me the chance for a big summer clear-out and to put together a new side. Oxford had two tremendous centre-halves in Gary Briggs and Malcolm Shotton, and I took Trevor Hebberd and George Lawrence from Southampton. My new strikers were Steve Biggins from Shrewsbury and Wrexham's Mick Vinter, whom I signed as a 16-year-old when I started a youth team at Boston United. He had scored six goals in a trial match I organised and after he signed for Boston I tried to get him to a League club. I was knocked back until Jimmy Sirrel took him to Notts County for a £50 donation. My mistake – County sold him to Wrexham for £120,000!

Our promotion miss that first season was quite dramatic as we went into our last three games needing three wins. The first of these was a midweek local derby at Swindon which prompted some amazing scenes. Fifteen minutes into the game, Swindon fans threw two smoke bombs into our penalty area. Our 'keeper, Roy Burton, was desperately trying to get the game stopped as the smoke began to swirl round his goal. The ball went out for a throw-in and the linesman flagged to point out the problem to the ref, but he ignored it and let play go on.

46

Ron Saunders . . . replaced me at Birmingham City

Through the smokey haze in front of our goal, Burton did not see the Swindon shot until it hit the back of the net. The protests of our players were waved away, but our fans were incensed and a shower of coins came on to the pitch – one of which hit the ref and laid him out. He recovered to continue with the game, but we ended up losing by that bizarre goal.

I was fuming afterwards and was ready to have my say when we heard that HMS *Sheffield* had gone down in the Falklands. When you put it into that perspective, missing out on promotion pales into insignificance.

Chapter 4

FROM OXFORD TO LONDON

A STRANGE DAY AT WEMBLEY

MANAGING Oxford United gave me some marvellous times. We won the Third Division Championship in 1984 – a season that also saw the club involved in 18 Cup-ties – and the next year we stormed to the Second Division title, taking the club into the top flight for the first time in its history.

Oxford is a small club, but it had a super family atmosphere and I felt I could have finished my career there – until things went wrong between myself and chairman Robert Maxwell.

In my first full season in charge we finished fifth, but I was all set to put the final touches to a Championship side. Bobby McDonald came in on a free at left-back and Steve Hardwick took over in goal.

We enjoyed a tremendous League Cup run that included beating mighty Manchester United over three games. We drew with them 2–2 at Oxford and 1–1 away and United were very keen to have the third game at Old Trafford. Ron Atkinson and Martin Edwards applied a bit of pressure to me, pointing out that we would make more money at Manchester and we were likely to lose anyway. I knocked it back because it was Robert Maxwell's decision, not mine.

In the end, we tossed for choice of venue over a phone line to the League headquarters, with Maxwell making the successful call. The decider went to extra time, but when Steve Biggins knocked in the only goal in front of our own fans, you could taste the elation. It was a truly wonderful moment.

In the quarter-final we faced Everton at a time when my pal Howard Kendall was in a very precarious position. There was a feeling in the game that if Oxford repeated their giant-killing act on Everton, then Kendall was on his way out of Goodison Park.

The game was at the Manor Ground and we were 1–0 up and bossing things with just ten minutes left. Kevin Brock was in possession, but he was being harried mercilessly by Peter Reid. I am still convinced that Reidy fouled him, but Kevin is too honest a player to go down – he wants to play football all the time. Under pressure, Brock knocked the ball blindly back to the 'keeper and Adrian Heath latched on to it and equalised. That goal saved the day for Everton and probably kept Kendall in a job. Brocky has taken a lot of stick for the slip, but we could still have won the tie in the last seconds had not Biggins headed over an open goal.

We lost the replay and I was at fault. I considered that we had beaten Everton at our place without getting the result and I felt confident enough to field a 4–2–4 formation at Goodison. It went wrong and they beat us, going on to the final where they lost to Liverpool. It was enough to keep Howard in a job and the following season he brought the Championship back to Goodison Park, deposing their great Mersey rivals.

As at most of my clubs, I did a lot of wheeling and dealing. One of the best pieces of business I ever did was netting John Aldridge from Newport for a mere £70,000. He went on to become one of the League's most prolific marksmen.

I also did well bringing in another striker, Billy Hamilton from Burnley, for £80,000. I rang Burnley's manager, John Bond, and asked about Hamilton. 'He'll score you 20-odd goals a season, but he cannot play!' was Bond's bizarre assessment. I have never understood what he meant, but over 20 goals for £80,000 sounded like a good deal to me. So it proved and it was a shame that injuries prevented him from playing as much as he would have liked. Hamilton was a better player than people give him credit for – a great pro and a joy to work with.

Aldo and Billy knocked in a lot of goals as we went through

Peter Reid . . . harried Kevin Brock mercilessly

the Second Division in a season that also saw Oxford put Arsenal out of the FA Cup. Other players I picked up during three years at the Manor Ground were Dave Langan on a free, Les Phillips for £5,000, and Trevor Hebberd as a makeweight in the deal that took Mark Wright to Southampton.

But I did not get it right all the time. I had signed Nigel Winterburn as a schoolboy at Birmingham and when they let him go I gave him a trial at Oxford. I always thought Nigel was going to be a very good player, but he had a nightmare time with us and I was happy to let him go to Wimbledon for nothing. Now he is one of the best left-backs in the country.

Two successive titles transformed Oxford into a football-oriented town, but my differences of opinion with the chairman meant I headed for Queen's Park Rangers – and their notorious plastic pitch – in the summer of 1985. It is one of my biggest regrets that I never managed Oxford in the First Division.

Working for Maxwell was always a stimulating experience and there was one point where his dealing could have seen me take control at Manchester United. It was in February 1984 and Maxwell was attempting to buy United from Martin Edwards. Press speculation suggested that if he was successful, he would instal me as manager at Old Trafford. It put me in an awkward spot, because Ron Atkinson was in charge of United. And while there was obvious appeal in running the glamour club of British football, I had to come out and say that I would be staying at Oxford and that United should retain Ron's services no matter who owned the club. As it turned out, Martin Edwards wanted £15 million and Maxwell was not prepared to stump up that kind of cash.

By the time Oxford kicked off their first match in Division One, I was behind the desk at Loftus Road and trying to exorcise the ghost of Terry Venables. He had left his mark indelibly etched on Rangers before heading out to fame and fortune with Barcelona. And replacing Venables had proved a problem for chairman Jim Gregory.

Alan Mullery had been brought in, but had been sacked after six months and Gregory had decided to run the team himself. A chairman-manager's role was right up his street! There had been an approach to Don Revie, who had been out in the

John Aldridge . . . one of my best ever buys

Middle East for seven years, and finally Frank Sibley came in as a caretaker. That obviously was not working too well because I ended up with the job.

Mullery reckoned he was let down by the players and that could have happened to me, too, because all the time I was there, Venables's name reverberated about the place. He was – and probably still is – looked on as a god. There was a lot of 'Terry did it this way' and 'Terry did it that way' and it created problems for me.

I do not know Venables well. He does not open out very much and the only contact you get from him is when he wants to do a deal – which is most of the time! He is the sort of bloke who comes up to you out of the blue at a dinner and asks if you will sell such-and-such. You say: 'OK, if the money is right', then off he goes and that is the last you hear of it.

I did not know Venables well, and the contact I had with him was when he wanted to do a deal. He is the sort of bloke who comes up to you at a do and asks you how much you want for

Oxford United – Third Division Champions 1984

54

At the Manor Ground after winning the Third Division Championship

a player. You say a figure and that's the last you hear of it. Venners used to bounce off managers to get the value of players.

So it was my job to sweep away the Venables system and one of the first things I did was stop them playing the offside trap. The lads were all keen on it – it was Terry's way – but I regard it as dangerous defensively and it goes against my beliefs about playing football.

Queen's Park Rangers is a strange club. It is a London club without the glamour and it only has a hardcore support of about 8,000. The rest only turn up for the big games or if the other London clubs are out of the capital. Despite having a super stadium, you never feel you are part of the community there – unlike in Oxford or Birmingham. Chairman Jim Gregory was a football nut, but his passion meant defeat was very hard for him to take. He was also a great wheeler and dealer, but his saving grace was that he always wanted people who could play with the ball.

I faced a difficult first season at Loftus Road and it was probably a successful run in the League Cup that swung things my way. It helped me win a few battles with the players and those that I still did not see eye-to-eye with were moved on.

That season, of course, also provided a great irony. I got Rangers to the League Cup final at Wembley and who should we meet but my old club Oxford! And the simple fact is that in my only Wembley appearance I felt closer to the opposition than to my own team.

It was an odd season for QPR because we struggled in the League and had to fight to stave off relegation. Yet in the League Cup, everything ran for us. We beat Hull 3–0 in a first-leg tie, but they were hammering us at their place and went a goal up. I thought: 'Here we go – we are on our way out here.' But every time we shot, we scored and ended up romping it 5–1.

Next up were Nottingham Forest at home. There was a snowstorm that night and the floodlights failed, but Cloughie was convinced it was one of Jim Gregory's tricks to get them in and out of the dressing-room and unsettle them. We could not get the lights going, but we got ourselves going in the rearranged game and won 3–1.

That left us with a derby game against Chelsea. We drew 1–1 at home and went to Stamford Bridge to be greeted by a typical Ken Bates article in the programme. The Chelsea chairman was his usual sweet-talking self – 'That plastic is diabolical, but now that we have got them at our place, we will stuff them!' Wrong again, Ken. We won 2–0 in extra time.

The semi-final pitted Rangers against Liverpool over two legs and we scraped a 1–0 victory at Loftus Road. At Anfield, Jan Molby missed a penalty for them before they went one-up . . . we equalised, but they got another. The match seemed destined for extra time, so I put sub Wayne Fereday on in the dying minutes to warm him up for the extra period. But, in the final seconds, he chased a long ball over the top, put Gary Gillespie under pressure and Gillespie obliged by scoring an own goal. We were at Wembley against an Oxford team that I had put together over the previous three years.

My only taste of managing a side at the national stadium was a strange, unreal experience. Something just did not seem quite right – and not just the fact that I had a greater affinity to the Oxford players and staff than my own lads at QPR. For one

Trying out for Lord Mayor after Oxford won the title in 1985

thing, you have to be at the stadium an hour-and-a-half before kick-off. You have a walk round the pitch and then go into these massive dressing-rooms where there are two blokes to look after you. It seemed a totally false situation to me and it was ages before we could actually get on with what we were there for – a game of football. I found it very hard to get things going with the Rangers players and such was the false feeling that I struggled to get them up for the off.

I still expected us to win the game – Oxford had hardly set the First Division alight – but we bottled it. Although we were the better team on paper, we just could not handle the big day.

Oxford United v Queen's Park Rangers is not exactly a glamorous League Cup final – or Milk Cup as it was known then – at least not in journalists' terms. The prospect had not got the media's pulses racing and I believe that, consequently, Oxford were cheated of the recognition they deserved. They played extremely well, even allowing for our poor display, and ran out 3–0 winners. Yet the response to their quality football was muted in the papers afterwards.

Man of the Match Trevor Hebberd got the first goal and then set up the second for Ray Houghton early in the second half. Jeremy Charles put the finishing touches to what was becoming a nightmare game for me. For the record, the teams in that 1986 final were *OXFORD*: Judge, Langan, Trewick, Phillips, Briggs, Shotton, Houghton, Aldridge, Charles, Hebberd, Brock. *QPR*: Barron, McDonald, Dawes, Neill, Wicks, Fenwick, Allen (Rosenior), James, Bannister, Byrne, Robinson.

I felt sick at the end and did not know where to put myself, but a lovely thing happened as I walked off towards the famous Wembley tunnel. The Oxford fans, who were gathered at that end, spontaneously started singing 'There's only one Jim Smith!' It was a very touching moment.

I went to congratulate the Oxford lads in their dressing-room and John Aldridge invited me to stay for a drink. I was feeling very down and not in the mood for a drink, but I sat with them for a while and chatted and finally Aldridge turned to me and said 'Don't worry – it's your team, boss.' There was an after-match dinner and I managed to put a face on for that, but my trip to Wembley took a lot of getting over.

At Wembley with QPR for the 1986 Milk Cup final

The next season at Loftus Road was a bit of a non-event. We had a poorish season, finishing 16th, and there was a time when I began to wonder if the ever-demanding Jim Gregory might not be going to give me the chop. As it happened, it was Gregory who went – not me. He sold the club he had built, to Marler Estates in February 1987 for £6 million.

David Bulstrode came in as chairman and I began to match the changes at the top with changes of my own. I moved Frank Sibley from assistant manager to youth team coach and brought in Peter Shreeve, who had been boss at Spurs, as my number two. I also decided to introduce the sweeper system and, with that in mind, signed Paul Parker for £200,000 – and what a good piece of business that has turned out to be!

The background staff at QPR were dead against using a sweeper and tried to argue me out of it, but I was not budging. We tried it out on the pre-season tour of Norway, with Parker operating in the right-back position where he has since made his mark for England in the World Cup. To be fair, he was not good enough then because his distribution of the ball was not up to what was required in the wide position. I had Terry Fenwick as a natural sweeper and I also bought John O'Neill from Leicester to play one of the central defensive roles.

Our first game of the new season was against West Ham who had a strike force of Tony Cottee and Frank McAvennie, both nippy little forwards. I knew I could not put O'Neill to man-mark either of those two as they would be too quick for him, so I pulled Parker inside to do a marking job on Cottee. Parker's assets are his speed and his tackling ability and he never gave Cottee a sniff as we won 3–0. In fact, Paul never gave anyone a smell that season. We topped the table after ten weeks and eventually finished fifth – my highest ever placing in the Football League.

We had a very promising side but, without a doubt, the sweeper system played a part in our success. I had to laugh at all the comments when England used a sweeper during the Italia '90 World Cup. It was treated as a revelation in the English game – as though Bobby Robson had just discovered it – but Lawrie McMenemy used it to good effect at Southampton even before I brought it in at Rangers. Other clubs have tried it but without conviction. It's no good just doing it for two or three games, you have to keep faith.

I believe that with the right players it is as good a system as anyone has so far dreamed up. The problem is the mentality of English players – when you play three defenders in the middle, you often end up with a back five. The full-backs should really be wide midfield men, who can do a bit of tackling, but can also get forward and cross the ball effectively. At QPR I had Parker as a central marker with Warren Neill coming in at right-back and Wayne Fereday, whom most people regarded as a winger, at left-back. Our best formation involved two front players and a winger – a sort of 3–4–3.

But you cannot play two wingers in the system and that presents a problem for England in that they will have to choose between John Barnes and Chris Waddle. In addition, I still prefer Parker as a central defender and I would play him along-side Des Walker with Trevor Steven, who is a quality crosser, at right-back.

Paul Parker was my best buy for QPR, along with 'keeper David Seaman, whom I snapped up for £200,000 from Birmingham. Both of them are now in the England squad and valued at over £1 million. Another good signing was taking Kevin Brock from my old club Oxford. But not all my moves were good ones. I was set to sign Tony Cascarino when he was leaving Gillingham, but changed my mind and went for Dean Coney instead. Dean did well for me, but he did not develop in the way that Cascarino did.

While we were the top-placed London club in the 1987–88 season, it was not all plain sailing. Marler Estates also owned Fulham's Craven Cottage and Chelsea's Stamford Bridge and they were particularly keen to sell Craven Cottage for the building of luxury homes. They came up with the plan to merge Fulham and QPR as Fulham Park Rangers and that caused a bit of a stink with the fans. At our home game with Manchester City there was a sit-down in the middle of the pitch – as it was Omniturf, it was quite good for sitting on! I had been through a similar thing with Robert Maxwell's Thames Valley Royals, so I knew it could turn nasty but, fortunately, things were settled quickly. There had been an even bigger demonstration at Fulham, and Marler agreed to sell out to Jimmy Hill's consortium.

Just before the end of that season I took Trevor Francis from Glasgow Rangers. Trevor may have been just short of his 34th birthday, but he still had the old skills I had first seen at Birmingham. At the start of the 1988–89 season, he was playing outstandingly well for us. But while things were going well on the pitch, there were difficulties off it.

David Bulstrode, with whom I had got on very well, had died and in came 23-year-old Richard Thompson. He was a nice lad, but I could sense things were going to get a little difficult with the new régime. We seemed to lose a bit of identity as a club and I began to feel uncomfortable.

When the approach came from Newcastle United, QPR were happy to let me talk to them, which probably says a lot. Richard Thompson asked me who should fill my seat at Loftus Road and I said they had to go for Peter Shreeve. They suggested Francis, but I said 'No' and unwittingly caused a bust-up with Trevor which took some time to heal. My reasoning was simple and honest. I did not doubt that one day Trevor would be a manager, but I knew that being a player-manager was the hardest job in football. My own experience told me how tough it was at a lower level and I regard it as virtually impossible to do successfully in the First Division. And, of course, Trevor was playing so very well and, in my opinion, was needed by QPR on the pitch. Having him as either manager or player-manager was bound to take something away from the team, therefore he was not the right choice.

But they offered the job to him and he asked me about it. I repeated what I had said to the chairman and it obviously upset Trevor, who was keen to try his hand at managing a side. My views forced a rift between us and we did not speak to each other for some time, although we are back on good terms now.

QPR actually put Peter Shreeve in charge until the end of the season but, two weeks later, he was moved out and Trevor Francis got the job. By that time, the manoeuvrings at Loftus Road were not my concern – I was up at Newcastle and facing some of the biggest nightmares of my career.

Chapter 5

HEARTBREAK AT NEWCASTLE

THE ONE THING THE FANS COULD
NEVER FORGIVE

IF I HAD known in advance of the two years of heartache I
faced when I moved to Newcastle United, I would not have
taken the job. Yet when the offer came, it was not a hard
decision to accept it. Here was a chance to take over at a big
club with tremendous potential . . . it was an opportunity to
test myself on a big stage and one I could not turn down. What
I did appreciate was how great the task was; how great the
expectation on Tyneside was; and how serious was the power
struggle which was enveloping St James's Park.

One of QPR's directors, Tony Ingham, asked me to recon-
sider just before I spoke to Newcastle – maybe I should have
listened to him. Instead, I met Newcastle chairman Gordon
McKeag in London on a Sunday in December 1988 and I was
in the North-East the next day. It was the quickest move I have
ever made.

My wife Yvonne was not over the moon about up-rooting
again and moving north. She has been amazingly understand-
ing about the demands of my chosen profession and we have
become quite expert at packing ourselves off to another part of
the country every few years. It is a hard fact of my life that I
have had to graft for a living and be prepared to move where
the work was. Yvonne had always tagged along uncomplain-
ingly. But after umpteen changes of address, Yvonne was reluc-
tant to move to Tyneside. We were settled in the south and had

our three grown-up daughters close by. Still, she appreciated I was not happy at Rangers and that I wanted a crack at a big club. It was my decision and she went along with it.

I knew Newcastle were having a bad time because I would not have been offered the job if that had not been the case. And I had read that they had gone after Arthur Cox and Howard Kendall and that David Hay had almost landed the job. But I had not done much homework on them – my gut feeling had again sat in judgement.

Gordon McKeag filled me in on the financial position – I would have to generate my own spending power – and on the Magpie Group, a consortium of businessmen engaged in a power struggle with the existing board. But other factors came to light as I got my feet under the desk . . . a number of fans were boycotting home games; the local newspaper was running a campaign to shift the balance of power at the club; and the team had played six straight League games without scoring a goal!

However those problems were temporarily shelved in my first match at home to Wimbledon. There was a great atmosphere at St James's Park and I got a marvellous welcome when I went out on to the pitch before the game. We had a fortunate 2–1 win, with John Hendrie ending the goal drought, and my feeling was that maybe the Magpie thing would not prove too serious. But when results started to go against us, the depth of feeling came out with a vengeance. And living in the North-East and seeing the local papers every day, I realised just how hot was the seat I sat in.

The Magpie Group was led by a developer called John Hall, a reputed millionaire who wielded a lot of influence in the region. They were involved in a share-buying campaign, which saw shares with a face value of fifty pence being bought for up to £2,000 each. Whether it was a takeover bid or not is open to debate, but it was certainly warfare of a kind between the board and the Magpie Group. With press support, John Hall had tapped into the disillusionment of the fans, who had seen little success at the club and Geordie stars like Chris Waddle, Peter Beardsley and Paul Gascoigne head for fresh pastures.

Newcastle United is one of the hottest jobs in the country because everyone there tells you what a great club they are. But

John Hendrie . . . got the winner in my first game at Newcastle

the truth is that Newcastle have not had a great football team for donkey's years. Even when they had three FA Cup wins in that golden era of the Fifties, they could not lift the Championship – and that is the measure of true greatness. But it is a big club with tremendous support and the supporters have looked at the Liverpools, Manchester Uniteds and Arsenals of the world and asked why it is not happening for Newcastle.

A common denominator is that at boardroom level it has often been the same family names and it was easy for someone like John Hall to exploit that fact. He got hold of the fans' frustration and disappointment and turned it against the directors. The fans will argue that they did not turn against the players or the club, but if there is so much hostility inside the ground it is going to affect players.

And the hostility built up over the remainder of the season and was instrumental in sending us down to the Second Division. Maybe if we had been good enough to win a few more of

65

those early games we could have turned the crowd around, but the squad I took over was lacking in several areas.

I brought in Bobby Saxton, who had recently quit York City, as my number two. I had known him from promotion battles between Oxford and Blackburn. Bobby had never worked in the First Division before and was a little apprehensive at dealing with players of that standard. I told him not to worry because the standard was nothing to be in awe of.

Although we beat Wimbledon in that opening match, I went out the next week and bought two full-backs, Kenny Sansom and Ray Ranson. There was no way the team that beat the Dons would have avoided relegation.

Kevin Brock had already arrived from QPR to signal the most hectic spell of buying and selling in my time as a manager.

Copyright: The Sunday Sun

Jim Smith with assistant Bobby Saxton

With Kevin Brock . . . my first signing for Newcastle

I knew drastic surgery was needed on the team and maybe I tried to do too much too quickly; I got caught up in the tension at the club and possibly over-reacted in the transfer market. Basically, I tried to do in a few months what needed two or three years to do.

But whatever I did, or whoever I signed, I could not prompt a permanent revival. And I do not blame the players who came in, because the feelings being generated towards the team at home games made it almost impossible to play. While some fans boycotted St James's, those who came made things very difficult for us. When you are in trouble, you need all the help you can get and a big plus in getting out of trouble can be the backing of your fans. In our battle to stay alive, our fans were a negative factor.

The players all put on a brave face going out for home matches, but at the end it was hate that was coming down from the terraces. And, of course, there were certain players singled out for extra treatment. There were demonstrations and scarf-burnings outside our ground and the atmosphere for our last game against Millwall when we were already down was as bad as any I have ever encountered.

At away games, oddly enough, we got excellent support and you could see how marvellous our fans could be. I suppose, if nothing else, the anger coming from the terraces at home showed just how passionate the fans were about Newcastle United.

Kenny Sansom came to Tyneside with over 70 caps, including outings as England skipper, yet he could not deal with the pressure. He had played all over the world and faced hostility from rival fans, but getting it from his own was a new experience and it got to him.

Ray Ranson and a Danish striker, Frank Pingel, were particular targets for the abuse. Pingel, who might not have made the grade anyway, at least showed bottle, put the shirt on and went out and tried while a few other players were prepared to make the most of minor knocks.

But while the players had to handle the aggro, the man who really took the stick was Gordon McKeag. He received hate mail and obscene and threatening phone calls, but he stood up to it all. Maybe he was a bit pig-headed about it, but I had to admire his courage. It made me want to do well, not just for the club and myself, but for him because if anyone deserves some success it is McKeag.

I, personally, did not have to take a lot of abuse and I retained faith in my ability to turn things round. Even at the height of a nightmare season, I got a lift when I arrived at the ground and saw 'NEWCASTLE UNITED' on the back of the lovely new Milburn Stand. It made me appreciate the potential at the club, and knowing that I had made the correct football decision to move there kept me sane.

Relegation obviously brought the Magpie campaign to some sort of peak and our strong promotion bid the following year saw a greatly improved atmosphere. We played some very entertaining football and the crowd seemed happy to give us a chance – especially after our 5–2 opening-day win against Leeds United, which saw Mick Quinn score four goals on his début.

Kenny Sansom . . . could not handle the pressure at Newcastle

Mick Quinn . . . four goals on his début against Leeds

On top of this, the warring factions were in a mood to bury the hatchet. I had always felt that if the money, know-how, commitment and emotion of the rival groups could be harnessed for the good of the club, then we could go places. And, thankfully, the directors and the Magpie Group moved towards the compromise that saw John Hall join the board in April, 1990.

A key part of the Magpie manifesto was turning Newcastle into a public company and selling shares to the ordinary fans – thus giving them some say in the affairs of the club. This has, of course, happened at Millwall, Tottenham and a few Scottish clubs – though with varying results. But now Newcastle United are embracing the notion of public ownership, I wonder what our supporters expect to get for holding a few shares? Do they expect the right to vote on who we sign, who we sell, who is the manager etc? I hope not, because in the end, Newcastle has to be run by a small body of men – the directors, the general manager and the manager. It is impossible for the ordinary fans to run the club and wrong for them to expect to have a say in decision-making. However, if they are buying shares as a gesture of support and to give those in power the chance to develop the club, then that is all right and it makes the responsibility of the board and the manager far greater. They must be seen to be doing everything possible to put Newcastle up there at the top.

When we went down to the Second Division, I was desperate to bounce straight back up as I had done with Birmingham City. The first objective was to break up the remnants of the old guard who had simply been at the club too long. Some of them had been there for five or six years and when you have the same old faces around it is easy to get stale. I needed fresh blood which would be motivated, and that meant another round of wheeling and dealing.

Because they were not what I wanted, or because we could cash in on them, the likes of Brazilian Mirandinha, John Hendrie, Michael O'Neill, Kenny Sansom and long-serving players David McCreery and Kenny Wharton all went. Another player to leave was Glenn Roeder, but that was because he was

Mirandinha and Dave Beasant (Wimbledon)

coming to the end of his career and looking to move into management. Glenn was out of the team and rather at odds with the club when I arrived, but I knew we needed his ability and experience and I restored him not only to the team, but also to the captaincy.

He did very well for me, as he had done for the club over some years. I just wish he had been five years younger – but then, I suppose, he wishes the same. Anyway, Glenn certainly showed the qualities which could, one day, make him a very good manager.

My team-building for the Second Division campaign saw me create a strike force of Mick Quinn and Mark McGhee, which was of crucial importance and which was to prove the best in the country in what ended up a heartbreak season. They knocked in 61 goals between them, with Quinny the League's top marksman on 36. Yet, there was an element of luck in them coming together.

I was tipped off about McGhee being interested in returning to Tyneside, but I did not have the chance to see him in 'live' action. I knew of his pedigree and saw enough on videos to realise he had great skills. And when I met him I got good vibes – he had been at Newcastle as a raw young lad and felt he had left the job unfinished – and at £200,000 from Celtic he was a bargain.

To be honest, Quinn was the bigger gamble and he was not my first choice. I wanted Wayne Clarke to partner McGhee, but he did not want to come. Quinn, with his drink-driving conviction and reputation as a Scouse scallywag who liked a bet, made me apprehensive and a few other players went through my mind before I returned to him.

Alan Ball, who had been Quinn's boss at Portsmouth, said there was not a better finisher and, as a World Cup winner, he had played with some of the greats. Other people I spoke to echoed those sentiments. Quinn's goals record was outstanding and I believe that players who are natural scorers will get goals at any level.

I still had some reservations, but signed him from Portsmouth with a tribunal setting the £680,000 fee – a figure I felt was a little over the odds. But it did not take long for me to realise he was a snip. He was what everyone had said – a super finisher.

Quinny is an ugly-duckling player . . . he looks awkward and unathletic. But he has more football ability than he shows because he is so single-minded about scoring and so anxious to get in the box – and that is where he is deadly.

There is no doubt that strikers work best in pairs and getting the chemistry right is vital. With a Scot and a Scouser I did just that. My team took shape for the promotion bid, but one thing that was badly needed at Newcastle United was a strong captain. The weight of expectation from the crowd is such that a formidable leader on the pitch is essential.

I gave the job to Kevin Dillon, whom I had signed from Portsmouth, but there were problems. Dillon is a bit of a moaner – though he has improved since I had him at Birmingham – and

Mick Quinn

I reckoned that one way to stop him moaning was to make him skipper. He did a good job as captain, but it affected his playing performances.

However, the main difficulty was that Kevin is from Sunderland and so great is the Newcastle–Sunderland rivalry that our fans would never take to him. I was unaware of how deep the North-East divide was when I signed him, otherwise I might not have bothered. I have sampled the rivalries between Birmingham City and Aston Villa; between Blackburn and Bury; and between Swindon and Oxford, but Newcastle and Sunderland is something else and it was quite a culture shock for me. The passion and antagonism between Tyne and Wear has been going on for years and we really felt its hot blast when we played Sunderland in the promotion play-offs.

Before that, though, I had resolved my captaincy problem by signing Roy Aitken, skipper of Scotland and Celtic. At £500,000, Roy had come a little expensive for a 31-year-old but I was investing in a leader as much as a player and I have been

73

tremendously impressed with him – both as a person and as a captain. He has no edge, commands respect by his mere presence and is as good a professional as I have ever worked with.

My move for Aitken prompted criticism that I was going for too many older players – that I was not giving youth a chance and so on. But that highlights one of the problems at United. The demand is for immediate success at St James's Park and we have to play with that kind of pressure. Older, experienced men are more likely to handle it, while younger players could easily be destroyed by it.

That season, 1989–90, we played some excellent football, scored more goals than any other team in the division and went into the final game still with a chance of the Championship. We lost that match to Middlesbrough and, after 46 games, found ourselves six points clear in third place. Yet we were not promoted. Instead, we had the dubious distinction of going into the play-offs with three teams shown not to be as good as us over a long, hard season.

The play-offs were originally introduced to reduce the size of the First Division and were then kept on as a money-making exercise, but to my mind they have no place in the Football League structure. The money made is shared between clubs not good enough even to make the play-offs and the notion of maintaining interest for more clubs towards the end of the season just rewards mediocrity.

Our play-off semi-final was against the old enemy, Sunderland, and that bit of local spice, added to the great prize at stake, made it a cauldron-like atmosphere for both legs.

The games had their share of drama and there was a feeling that here was a powderkeg waiting to go off.

In the first game at Roker Park there was a penalty save and a man sent off as the 90 minutes ended goalless. Back at St James's Park we had our chances, but Sunderland deservedly beat us 2–0 and when Marco Gabbiadini got the second it was the signal for our fans to invade the pitch. World Cup referee George Courtney was forced to take the players off for quite some time while order was restored.

It was not a particularly violent episode, mainly young kids running around, presumably trying to have the game

Roy Aitken joins Newcastle United

abandoned. But it did no favours for the image of the game or of Newcastle United to see a line of police and dogs marching across the pitch to deal with the trouble-makers.

It was a sickening occasion for me, but, in fact, I felt more for the players. The truth was that they had had a very good season and now here they were branded as failures. All the good football and thrilling goals that had filled 46 games were forgotten. That one game with Sunderland was a make-or-break for the season and, of course, it was made doubly worse for our fans in that it was the loathed red-and-whites who turned the knife. I think they could forgive us anything . . . except losing to Sunderland.

When the game was finally concluded, my players were abused and even spat at by a small section of their own supporters, instead of getting the credit they deserved for a very good season.

That night my emotions were in turmoil and I really could not think straight. Yvonne tried to console me and Ron Atkinson phoned me to commiserate. It was a full two days later when it really sank in and it felt worse than when we had been relegated the year before. At the end of the day, we knew we needed a top-two place to ensure a trip back to the First Division and we were not good enough to secure that.

But while everyone at St James's Park was gutted, it made me more determined than ever to see the job through. I had had the chance to leave the club that season when I had an unofficial approach to see if I was interested in the Manchester City job after Mel Machin had been sacked. City were bottom of the First Division, so it was not going to be an easy task and I had

Ecstasy for Alex Ferguson as Manchester United put Newcastle out of the FA Cup

just had a basinful of relegation with Newcastle. But that was not why I said I was not interested. Basically, I had come to Newcastle because here was the potential for me to achieve everything I wanted to achieve as a manager. When you take charge at Newcastle United, there is no need to move anywhere else. Whether the people there have the patience to stick with you is, I suppose, another matter.

I might also have replaced Graham Taylor at Aston Villa when he took over as England supremo. Villa chairman Doug Ellis asked Gordon McKeag for permission to talk to me and was refused – a decision I am quite happy with. There was a final irony to a season of despair . . . I won the Manager of the Month award. It was my first such award for Newcastle – I hope it is not my last.

Chapter 6

THE SELLING OF TREVOR FRANCIS

A CUDDLE FROM CLOUGHIE

I WILL always be known as the man who sold Britain's first £1 million-player – the supremely talented Trevor Francis. But the fact is, it never happened . . . Trevor moved from Birmingham City to Nottingham Forest for £1 short of the magic million mark.

I first met Trevor when I took over at Birmingham in March 1978. The team were battling against relegation and 23-year-old Trevor was in dispute with the club and looking for a move. He had spent a large part of his spectacularly successful career as the lone star in a struggling side. They were again bottom of the First Division and a long way from challenging for the honours that Francis craved.

It was my job to keep the club in the top flight and that meant harnessing Trevor's abilities. I had a long chat with him at the Holiday Inn before a match against Newcastle and he agreed to see how things went while I tried to improve the situation.

Things went well – we had only lost one of the last 16 games of the season and finished midway up the table. Trevor was outstanding and scored nine goals during that run.

Before I moved to the Midlands, City had had a £600,000-bid for Francis from the American club Minnesota Kicks, whose boss was ex-Birmingham manager Freddie Goodwin. It was turned down but, at the end of the season, Freddie came back to me trying to get Trevor on loan for the American summer season. Trevor was keen to go and was prepared to sign a new contract for us if I okayed the loan deal. Obviously that was good news for me, so I gave the loan my blessing and a verbal agreement was made with Goodwin.

But the story got out and appeared in a Sunday newspaper. I think the leak came via Goodwin and, if that is so, he had made a big mistake.

Straight away I got a call from Jimmy Hill, who was Coventry City's managing director and was also involved with Detroit Express in the USA. Francis had not yet signed a deal with Minnesota, and Hill was ready to nip in ahead of them and land him for Detroit.

Hill offered to double the money for a summer's work and that was enough to tempt the player. It was arranged that we would meet Hill at his farm in the Cotswolds and Trevor would sign there.

But two days before the deal was due to go through there was another twist. I got a call from Charlton Athletic manager Andy Nelson, whose chairman, a bloke called Glickstein, was behind Boston Teamen. I told Andy about the deal with Hill, but it transpired that Glickstein also had a farm in the Cotswolds and Trevor agreed to go there on the morning that he was due to sign for Detroit.

At Glickstein's farm we were told that Boston were ready to up the Detroit Express offer to a package worth £75,000 – a hell of a lot of money for three months' work.

As we drove the ten miles to Jimmy Hill's place, Trevor asked my views on the move. I pointed out that Boston was probably a nicer place to live than Detroit and that as one of the biggest companies in the world, Lipton's, was behind the Teamen, it was likely to be the sounder bet.

We arrived at the farm to find Detroit manager Ken Furphy there, plus a couple of the club's directors who had flown over from the States especially to meet their new star. They had champagne laid on and the works and yet Trevor was on the point of turning them down.

I quickly grabbed Jimmy Hill and pulled him into another room to inform him that Boston had just topped his offer. Jimmy is a professional man and he knew that, at the end of the day, it was about money. After all, he had stepped in when Freddie Goodwin had the deal lined up.

Detroit had pushed the boat out to come up with their offer and now they were going to have to push it out a little more. There was a long deliberation between Hill and his directors, but they finally stumped up the extra cash to match the Boston bid.

And so Trevor pocketed his £75,000 and spent the summer with Detroit Express. It had been a fascinating day for me – not least just listening to the figures being bandied about.

Francis was the first current international to go on loan to the States and he became very well known over there. I was pleased with the deal because it meant that he signed a new two-year contract with Birmingham and I was able to face the new season with optimism.

But, the sad truth is that it rebounded on me because he only got back from the USA on the Thursday before our new season kicked off. He looked tired and jaded and, as the other lads had done well in pre-season games, I made him sub for our opener against Manchester United.

He came into the side for our second game, but we made a bad start and were struggling generally. On top of that, his trip to the States, with all its attendant razzmatazz and the money on offer, had whetted his appetite for a bigger stage than Birmingham City were able to provide.

I had known there was an element of a gamble in letting him go abroad, but it had seemed the best move. However, things were not working out too well. We were due to play Liverpool and I decided to leave him out and suggested he took a week off to rediscover his old spark. Typically of Trevor, he still insisted on coming in and training, although I would have preferred him to rest.

During a training session he damaged his Achilles' tendon and missed the next 14 League games. Our season turned sour and he ended up only playing eight matches, scoring just three goals.

If we had done well on the park, I think I might have persuaded Trevor to see out his contract. It did, after all, make him about the highest-paid player in Britain, on something like

Jimmy Hill . . . wanted Trevor Francis for the United States

£40,000 a year. But he knew he was looking at another season of struggle and wanted away. You could not blame him – he had given Birmingham City good service over a number of years and now he was hungry for bigger and better things.

Word that he was unsettled quickly got round and in January 1979 Coventry City lodged a British record-breaking £900,000 bid. The board voted to turn it down, but even they were beginning to accept that we would have to cash in on our finest asset. When it was agreed to put Trevor on the transfer list a few weeks later, I sat down with the directors to discuss the fee and we settled for £1 million.

Word had it that Brian Clough fancied buying Francis, so I went to watch Nottingham Forest play Brighton in a League Cup quarter-final tie.

I was less interested in the game than in whether Cloughie was ready to do a deal. I waited around for a while after the game and was just about to go when he came strolling up to me, put his arms around me and gave me a big cuddle. It was in sharp contrast to our first meeting when Forest were in the Second Division and I was at Blackburn – then he would not talk to me, though I never found out why. But here he was with a cuddle and an invitation to Forest's League Cup semi-final first leg against Watford, when Trevor Francis would be on the agenda.

I arrived at 5.30 p.m. to be welcomed by Cloughie's right-hand man, Peter Taylor. I told him we wanted £1 million or £800,000 plus Forest's reserve 'keeper, Chris Woods (now of England and Rangers), and Steve Burke, an England Youth winger. Peter and I chatted for some time, but it was 6.55 p.m. before Clough appeared. They tried a bit of a double act to get me to reduce the asking price, but I was not budging – I already had Coventry's offer in the bag.

I remember looking at my watch. It was 7.20 p.m., ten minutes to kick-off, so I said to Brian: 'You've got to go see to your team, haven't you?'

His comment was: 'Stuff them – they know what they've got to do.'

He and Taylor finally left me at 7.23 to head for the dressing-room. It was a novel management approach to a big game, but

Trevor Francis . . . teenage star at Birmingham City

they sent their team out to a 3–1 win.

We still had not done a deal and there were a lot of newspaper men there eager to report a new British transfer record. Cloughie went out to speak to them and said I was this, that and the other and he could not do business with me. But a few days later Peter Taylor phoned me.

'Nine hundred and ninety-nine thousand nine hundred and ninety-nine pounds and that's it. We don't want him to become big-headed so we aren't going to give you a million.'

I said I was happy and the deal was tied up in a couple of minutes.

England were just about to kick-off against Northern Ireland on the TV and Taylor, who is famous for his love of a bet, asked me whom I fancied. I plumped for Ireland, but England won it and Taylor chased me for his £20, finally catching up with me on the last day of the season.

It is strange that Cloughie had played so little a part in the biggest transfer Britain had ever seen, but that is his style. It was also typical of the man that he was playing squash when Taylor met Trevor Francis to talk personal terms.

Shortly after I had agreed the deal with Taylor, Forest's chairman, Mr McPherson, rang my chairman, Keith Coombs, to ask if it was true that they had paid £1 million for Trevor. I don't think he had ever been consulted on the matter! In fact, with VAT and Francis's five per cent cut, the transfer – which was concluded on 10 February 1979 – was costing Forest over £1.1 million. And while that was an astonishing figure back then, I have to say that he was worth it. He was a superb player and, of course, he went on to score the winner for Forest in the European Cup final.

Eight years later, it was my turn to sign Trevor Francis and the fee had come down quite a bit . . . to £25,000 to be exact. From Forest he had gone to Manchester City, Sampdoria, Atalanta and then Rangers, from where I brought him to Queen's Park Rangers. Obviously, he did not have the sharp-ness of old, but he was still a quality player and his years in Italy had clearly influenced his thinking. He had developed an ultra-professional approach, which some people might think a bit over the top. From being a young lad who just played football,

Brian Clough . . . paid a record fee for Francis

he had become a student of the game. He always made sure he ate the right things and had a daily diet worked out and he also used a system of Italian warm-up routines, which were very good. He always was a very disciplined person – not one for heavy drinking or night clubs, he can come over as slightly cold and aloof, but when you get to know him he is a warm lad who likes a laugh.

When I left QPR, he was playing as well as anyone in the team. He could not get the goals he used to because he was not as quick in the box, but the ability was still there and he had a much greater awareness.

No doubt his thoughts had turned to management, for he had seen what had been achieved by his contemporaries Kenny Dalglish and Graeme Souness. But when he was made player-manager at Loftus Road, he immediately hit problems in making the transition from team-mate to boss. You have to be a special man to go from being one of the players to taking charge – it is very difficult.

His lack of experience in the job showed up when, curiously enough, he brought QPR up to the North-East to play against the Newcastle team I had just taken over. Included in the squad was Martin Allen who quit the team hotel on the Friday and headed back to London to see his wife give birth. Trevor fined him and I understand the point he was trying to make, but if it had been me I would not have taken Allen up to Newcastle. He had been out injured and so was not likely to make the starting line-up. I would also have kept any disciplinary action a lot quieter so that it did not get blown out of proportion – as happened with the Allen incident.

I must say that in my day as a player no one would have dreamed of missing out on a first-team game and possible win, just to see their son or daughter born. But times change and maybe in the modern world that is the wrong attitude.

Trevor was sacked after 11 months as boss of Rangers and difficulties with players was cited as the reason. He is a singular man who knows his own mind and can be rather unbending. But when you are manager to 30 professionals, you have to bend sometimes even if you don't want to. Maybe Trevor could not do that. But I know he will learn from his mistakes and could make a very good manager if he decides to have another go.

The money Birmingham City got from the Francis deal enabled me to go out and buy a number of good players . . . and there were quite a few characters among them.

Little Archie Gemmill came from Forest and I made him captain for his ability, experience and also because he was so demanding of other players on the pitch, which was what I wanted. He did upset a number of the younger players, like Mark Dennis and Kevin Dillon, with his verbal lashings. But I think they would both now admit that Archie's attitude was spot on.

Another player I signed was the mercurial and highly individual Frank Worthington, who came to us from Bolton Wanderers. I went to meet Frank to discuss the deal at the home of Bolton director Brian Turnbull. We quickly came to an agreement and drank and chatted through the night and I recall driving along the M6 next day thinking: 'Christ, I've just signed a bloke who drank more whisky than me last night!'

But I had done my homework on Worthy and people like George Mulhall and Ian Greaves had told me that, whatever I read about his wild lifestyle, he was never a problem as a player. And that is how it proved to be.

Because of his flamboyant dress and the fact that he loved a party, people got the wrong impression of Frank. He was a super lad and a super talent. He liked a few bevvies, but he never let it affect his game because he loved playing and took great pride in his performance. He had tremendous natural gifts and when he went out on the park he wanted to show he was the best player there.

He did not like all the running about much in training, but give him the ball and he would have stayed there all day. After training he would get two apprentices and have one knock balls across while he buried them past the other in goal. On a Friday, I used to have to drag him off the training ground.

I will always remember his arrival at Birmingham – it was a freezing cold day and Frank turned up in sunglasses, tight jeans, cowboy boots and a jerkin with some rock-'n'-roll band's world tour announced on the back.

I took him to meet the other players pretending he was blind. 'Watch the door, Frank . . . be careful there's a step' etc. Keith Bertschin complained: 'You are taking the mickey out of him already, boss.' But Frank just looked at the lads through his shades and said: 'Don't worrry babies, it's like water off a duck's back.'

I always felt Worthy was unlucky in that he was about to sign for Liverpool, but failed the medical because of high blood pressure. He had been away for a fortnight in Majorca and just stepped off the plane before heading for Anfield – knowing Frank, after two weeks in Majorca, I would expect his blood pressure to be up a little. If he had signed for Liverpool, I think he might have established himself as an England striker for many years.

Colin Todd, a genius of a defender, was another one of the new Birmingham recruits. He has a tremendous physique, a great brain and lightning pace, and always says the biggest regret of his career is turning down the England captaincy – but I can imagine him doing it. He was always a quiet lad who preferred to concentrate on his own job.

He could be moody, too, if we were up against a Shrewsbury or a Cambridge when it was the beginning of the up-and-under long-ball style that has become so fashionable. That was not football to him – he could not stand that style – and he would be less effective in those games. But give him a big game against top-quality opposition and he was world class.

One of the funniest characters we had at Birmingham was Dave Langan, an Irish full-back whom I bought from Derby. Dave had this obsession about nicknaming every player and, not just content with giving them the name, he insisted on using it all the time – even during matches. So he would be shouting: 'Pass it to me, Six Million Dollar Man (Colin Todd)', or 'Over here, Idiot (Mark Dennis)'. He dubbed Archie Gemmill 'Mr Angry' though later on I became 'Mr Angry'.

I took Langan to Oxford with me and when I said in the papers that John Aldridge scored goals like Jimmy Greaves, Aldridge became 'Greavsie'. We also had 'Nijinsky' (Trevor Hebberd) and 'The Drunkard' (Les Phillips). Oddly enough, I don't remember Langan ever having a nickname himself. Another signing during my time at St Andrews was 'keeper Tony Coton, whom I snapped up for £1,000 from non-League Mile Oak. He was a quiet lad and very insecure and my coaching staff told me he would never make the grade and that we should get rid of him. But I still rated him and over-ruled them.

He made his début against Sunderland and created some sort of a record because his first touch in a League game was a

Policing the sidelines

penalty save, inside the first half-minute. Coton is now one of the best 'keepers in the country and pushing for a place in the England squad.

Not all my signings have been inspired, but then, when you have done as many deals as I have, there are bound to be some that do not work out. Strikers Neil Whatmore and Alan Buckley, both of whom I brought to Birmingham, were less than successful for me. But overall I think my record stands up to scrutiny and I do feel that ability in the transfer market is a major factor in judging a manager.

One of my best ever deals was John Aldridge, whom I took to Oxford from Newport County.

Aldo had been playing with South Liverpool and had been spotted by the brother of Len Ashurst who was in charge at Newport. Len had signed him on and then left and taken over at Sunderland. He wanted to take Aldridge to Roker Park, but he could not come up with the money. Newport wanted £80,000 but my chairman at Oxford, Robert Maxwell, stepped in with £70,000 up front to clinch it.

A typically bubbly Scouser and a bit of a scallywag, John was not blessed with overenthusiasm for training, but once a match kicked off he would come alive and his awareness in front of goal was brilliant.

I made a mistake in not taking him to Queen's Park Rangers when I moved there. I had a question mark over whether he could do it in the First Division which I should never have had – natural scorers like John will get goals in any division.

Another outstanding investment was Dave Wagstaffe, who joined me at Blackburn for just £3,000 from Wolves.

Waggy was possibly the most talented player I have ever managed, but he suffered from a terrible nervous problem. He smoked heavily and some days he just could not face the world. He would miss training when the nerves were too bad, but on other days – at the age of 33 – he would run everyone else off the park.

Once, we were playing Burnley in a Boxing Day derby in front of 33,000 fans and Wagstaffe could not go out – his nerves were shot. I was ready to give him a hard blast of the verbals, but my assistant, Norman Bodell, who had been with Waggy at Wolves, went and got the club doctor who gave him some tablets. They were just aspirin really, but Dave was suddenly feeling all right and went out and played out of his skin.

We were 3–0 up at half-time when Waggy walked in and announced that he could not face the second half! It was time to get out the aspirin again, and a revived Dave went out after the break and showed himself to be the best player on the park.

Chapter 7

MIRANDINHA, TARANTINI
AND MARK DENNIS

THE BOY FROM BRAZIL

FRANCISCO Ernani Lima da Silva – better known as Mirandinha – is the man who could have kept Newcastle United in the First Division during my first season on Tyneside. He was the one with the extra-special talent, the little bit of magic that could have got us out of the hole we were in. And if he had produced it regularly, rather than occasionally, we would not have suffered the sickening relegation in 1989.

When I arrived at Newcastle in December 1988, I was warned that one of my biggest tasks would be to solve the riddle of the enigmatic Mirandinha . . . to get him to turn it on week in, week out. In the end, I have to say that it was one task I could not handle – though, Lord knows, I tried everything I could think of.

Mirandinha made history when he signed for Newcastle from Palmeiras in August 1987 by becoming the first Brazilian to play in the Football League. His first season was, by all accounts, a hit-and-miss affair in which he thrilled and disappointed in equal measure. He was the club's leading scorer, but failed to complete the season.

When I eased myself into the manager's chair at St James's Park, the team was bottom of Division One. Mira was the big name and, according to some, the big problem.

The first thing I noticed about him in training was how he

92

Mirandinha

could not find the back of the net. In practice games and even in unopposed sessions he would miss goals you would not believe. Then he would suddenly unleash a blistering drive that was unstoppable. And that was the story of the season.

My dilemma was that I never knew if he wanted to play for Newcastle. I would talk to him, tell him what I wanted and be convinced that he was on our side, but then something would happen when he went out on the pitch.

There were times when he asked for a transfer, claiming his agents had fixed him up with a move to Spain or Portugal, and then he would leave my office and go outside and tell the waiting reporters that he was very happy and wanted to stay with Newcastle. One of Mira's problems was that he wanted to be everyone's friend – he was on his own a long way from home and he tried to be all things to all people.

He always had money worries – he felt he had been let down by his agents in the past – and he always had family trouble back in Brazil. The family were running his pig farm over there and that seemed to be one big personal and financial headache. I did not get the brunt of all these problems – they landed on the desk of our general manager Russell Cushing.

My problem was out on the pitch and getting him to complete 90 minutes. Sometimes you had to pull him off because he just was not doing it and other times he would come off injured. In fact, for an injured man he could get off the park pretty quickly as I found out in a game against Middlesbrough at Ayresome Park. He had made a storming start and had set up a goal for Liam O'Brien to put us one up. Then he went down in a tackle and got up limping. I was in the directors' box and thought: 'I had better get down there sharpish or he's going to come off.' I dashed down from the box, but Mirandinha was always faster than me and, as I reached the tunnel, he came running past me. He had taken himself off and we ended up with a 1–1 draw from a game we should have won.

We played Watford in a long-running FA Cup third-round tie and in the first replay Mira was terrorising their defence with his pace. We went a goal down, but he equalised and then helped put us ahead as he continued to scare the life out of big John McClelland. Next thing I know he says he is injured and

Mirandinha . . . Newcastle's enigmatic Brazilian star

comes off. I asked him if he had pulled a muscle or something serious, but he said: 'No, I think I have cramp.'

You would not let a British player come off with cramp. It is the sort of thing you would sort out with treatment on the pitch and get him going again. We eventually lost to Watford at the fourth attempt, through a Glenn Roeder own goal. Those four Cup-ties cost us dear in terms of wear and tear for the League campaign.

It seems that Latin players have a different mentality to injuries than we do. Certainly Mira had a very low pain threshold and that reflected one of the major difficulties he had in adapting to life in the Football League. Here you usually have to battle for 90 minutes and almost every match is highly competitive. Mirandinha was used to a league where he had quite a few easy games each season, games that Palmeiras were going to coast through.

He was also used to a less concentrated programme and he found the demands of competing physically twice a week very hard to deal with. While he had the ability to escape tight marking, he did not relish the physical challenges.

Of course, he was with us at a bad time – the team was in dire straits and he was not a man used to relegation battles. He had the talent to help us survive, but he did not have the stomach for the scrap and that is what is needed when you are on the bottom.

I worked very hard on him. I tried to make him less selfish and I persuaded him to play further upfield, rather than dropping back and losing possession in dangerous areas. I put my arm around him plenty of times and I also gave him a few kicks up the backside. But neither method could guarantee a consistent level of performance.

The crunch for our season came after we had beaten Everton at St James's and then had a great win at Norwich. Mira was playing well and I thought we had turned the corner, that we were going to stay up. We then met fellow-strugglers Sheffield Wednesday at home on Easter Monday and lost disastrously. The next game was at Southampton, who were also in relegation trouble. Both teams were poor, but Mirandinha had three chances to win it for us and fluffed them. I just felt he had given up on us after the Sheffield Wednesday defeat. He seemed to lose interest at a time when we needed players to roll up their sleeves and battle. He had accepted we were going down and, again, he did not see out the season.

People have said that I was against Mira, but that is not true. I got on with him all right, but in the end I could not respect him as a professional.

There are obvious pitfalls in bringing a South American over to Britain and a key one is that it works against team spirit. Mirandinha wanted this, he wanted that and it sometimes seemed as if everything had to be geared around him. Imports tend to regard themselves as superstars – though they may not really merit that accolade – and expect to be treated accordingly. Naturally, you have to cater for them and look after them. They are on their own and have no group of mates to rely on. But it can be divisive in the dressing-room and I don't think the other lads were too unhappy when Mira went for good.

He also got himself into situations by talking to the Press. He was a godsend to reporters . . . they kept ringing him up and he kept saying what they wanted to hear. Sometimes he felt I did not understand him; sometimes the board were against him; sometimes he felt people were trying to force him out of Newcastle. He once said that the club treated the players like second-class citizens – that they had fish and chips, while the directors smoked fat cigars.

For a start, none of the directors smoked and often players – and Liverpool do this – want fish and chips after a game so they can get away quickly and get home. I know that story was put into his head by a reporter. Mira was big news and the Press used him and that is why I have some sympathy for him.

The news hounds were always ready to pull out the excuse that they had misunderstood him; that there was a mix-up over languages. Don't you believe it! Mirandinha could talk excellent English when he wanted, just as he could struggle with the language when it suited him. During one long chat, he was telling me about his money problems, his stocks and shares and the financial markets – he spoke better English than me!

Accepting that Mira came to the club at an awkward time, you still have to regard the transfer as a failure. Nevertheless, he excited the crowd in his few fantastic individual moments. The Newcastle public love players with pace and power and he became a hero in the tradition – though not in the same esteem – of Jackie Milburn, Malcolm Macdonald and Kevin Keegan.

The fans took to Mirandinha even when he was bad because of his style. Yet, amazingly, at first they did not take to Mick Quinn, whom I bought to replace the Brazilian. And that is even though Quinny scored four on his début and week in, week out will give you a much better return than Mirandinha.

Mira's two years on Tyneside – a bamboozling mixture of magic and moodiness – came to an end when we loaned him back to Palmeiras for the 1989–90 season. He was quite content with the deal but, just before he signed, another club came in offering him more money and United a bit less. Mira was all set to renege on his verbal agreement with Palmeiras until their president, who was a senior official in the Brazilian FA, suggested that his future in Brazil was on the line unless he stuck with Palmeiras. So he signed for them and at the end of the loan period we sold him to them permanently. A year later he announced that he wanted to come back, but he was a bit older and I was a bit wiser. In any case, Palmeiras wanted three times more than we had sold him for!

Mira was not my first taste of the problems peculiar to Latin players trying to make their mark in British football . . . I had also had Alberto Tarantini at Birmingham.

Tarantini was a World Cup winner with Argentina in the summer of 1978 and later that year he followed compatriots Osvaldo Ardiles and Ricardo Villa into the Football League in deals organised by Harry Haslam. But while Ardiles and Villa went to Spurs to receive the acclaim of the national Press, Alberto came to less fashionable Birmingham and struggled to get a fair deal from the media.

I bought him for £250,000 from Boca Juniors and, while he was known as a tough defender, he also had amazing skill. I remember almost 1,000 people turning up just to watch him training. But the London reporters seemed to have a preconceived idea about him and they were not very complimentary.

We played Spurs and, of course, afterwards he linked up with Ossie and Ricky who told him what a great time they were

Mirandinha

having. Alberto came up to me and said: 'Boss, why me? Why always me who has problems and get criticised? Boy just come up to us for autograph and Villa did not know word "pen" – Villa a donkey; I'm OK!'

To be fair, Tarantini did not really perform for us. Like Mirandinha, he was faced with the problem of settling in to a struggling team and, while he had bags of talent, it was only seen occasionally. One of those occasions was against Coventry when he was brilliant. Joe Mercer asked me to introduce him to Alberto – Joe said it was one of the best performances he had ever seen.

But Tarantini also carried a bit of a hard-man reputation around with him – a reputation that was not helped by an incident during a game against Manchester United. We had a big win over the Reds, but all the attention was focused on a clash between Alberto and Brian Greenhoff. Greenhoff ended up on the deck and was carried off. Everyone said that Tarantini had thumped him, but when quizzed by the Press Tarantini explained what had happened: 'No, I did not hit him – he was just tired.' In fact, he was not a tough guy at all, but he did get bad publicity for getting sent off and the difference between his treatment and that of Ardiles and Villa made it all the more difficult to settle.

On a personal level, I got on with him very well and used to love his attempts to master the English language. Once we played a charity game in the freezing cold at Newport and afterwards he pointed at his toes and said: 'Boss, my fingers are so cold', because in Spanish it is the same word for toes and fingers.

But things were not going well at the club, so when an offer for Tarantini came in from Cordoba the board were very keen to take it. I would have liked to have hung on to him and chairman Keith Coombs felt the same way, but the vote went against us.

The final game of the season saw the officials from Cordoba arriving to sign him up, but there was one problem – Alberto did not want to go. He had become very fond of life in England and he pleaded with me to keep him. He asked me to tell the Cordoban entourage that the deal was off, but my hands were

Alberto Tarantini . . . World Cup winner with Argentina

tied so I said: 'If you tell them you don't want to sign for them, that is fine by me.' But Tarantini pointed out that the president of Cordoba was also the head man in the Argentinian FA and if he openly defied them he would never play for his country again. The transfer went ahead and we got £230,000 back, so I do not regard his signing as the disaster some people have since painted it. But there were always arguments over Tarantini – I really rated him, yet people such as Ron Atkinson and John Bond insisted he could not play.

A year after we sold him we got promoted back into the First Division and I bumped into him in London after the England v Argentina match. He said: 'When I was at Birmingham . . . bad team. Now good team – why not me there, boss?'

One of the players in what was becoming a very good Birmingham team was Mark Dennis, a one-off who – like the two famous imports – brought his own particular problems.

Mark has got a wild-man reputation which he has been unable to shake off and, to be fair, he certainly earned it. The first time I ever crossed swords with him I had to fine him for being sent off in a junior game. He was 16 then and already a bit of a tearaway, but his ability was such that a year later he made his first team début . . . in unusual circumstances. I brought him into the squad and named him as sub at Norwich. But our full-back Jimmy Calderwood went to the toilet before the game with his boots on, slipped on the tiles and hurt his back, so Dennis had to start in his place. We lost the game 4–0, but he was never out of the side after that.

In those days he was hyperactive. On a pre-season tour to Sweden he trained morning and after lunch, played tennis late afternoon, then went on to darts and billiards all evening. He did not wake up for training the next day!

A loveable rogue, he is a very good player, one of the best crossers on the run that I have seen and was up alongside Kenny Sansom as a left-back during the 1980s. But, although he is a Youth and Under-23 international, he has never won a full England cap and that is a crime. His abysmal disciplinary record has, of course, weighed heavily against him where England is concerned and, in that sense, he has wasted his talent.

Ossie Ardiles . . . well-received by the British Press

He has also wasted his talent by getting sent off and suspended when he should have been playing, but he has a crazy, self-destruct button that he must push. In one game we were four goals to the good against Southampton with just five minutes left when Alan Ball made a run down the right and tried to take Dennis on. Bally tried to get his cross in, but kicked the turf instead and the ball trickled away for a goal kick. That was the signal for Dennis to start giving out some lip – it is in his nature to want to wind people up. He said Ball was 'washed-up' and 'a has-been' and Bally being Bally he retaliated and they both got sent off, which was ridiculous with the game dead as a contest and only minutes from the end.

Mark's mouth was his big problem – he just could not keep it shut. But he also had a tendency to whack the opposition because he was basically not a good tackler and would often dive in and catch players late. He was no different on the training pitch when he would happily give his own team-mates a blast of the verbals and a boot. Yet he is a great lad in the dressing-room – he is bubbly, a good laugh and desperately wants to win.

The day we got promotion from the Second Division in a match against Notts County, Mark was suspended for a change. But he was so wound up for the other lads that after 20 minutes watching from the stand he could not take the tension anymore. He left and walked around the ground until the game was over and that illustrated to me his tremendous desire for success. The problem is he wants to win too badly on occasions.

He could be quiet as a mouse one moment and then suddenly all hell would break loose. I would get him into my office and by the time he left I would be convinced that he was right and I was wrong. He would sit there with his angelic face saying: 'I didn't do anything' or 'It was the ref's fault' and you ended up feeling sorry for him and being sure he was an innocent victim of a miscarriage of justice.

I had plenty of bust-ups with him, but there **was** never any on-going bad feeling. I would lose my temper and blow my top, but it was accepted that things were just said in the heat of the moment – after all, that was often his excuse when he had mouthed it off to a ref. I made numerous attempts to sort Dennis out, but it is a fact that you could never really alter him.

Mark Dennis . . . kept hitting the self-destruct button

I fined him heavily and I had long chats with him, but what is in his nature is there to stay.

In the early days, after I had had him in the office, I would be convinced that I had sorted the Mark Dennis problems out once and for all. But I learned the hard way that you can never sort him out. The only solution, in the end, was to sell him as I had Nigel Winterburn coming through at St Andrews. However, I did not get the immediate offer I was looking for and before I could get rid of him, I was shown the door by the club. Ron Saunders, who replaced me, reckoned he was going to sort out Mark Dennis and Birmingham's disciplinary problems, but he had even less success than me.

Five years after I was sacked I bought Dennis for QPR from Southampton for just £20,000. I thought that he must have matured a bit since the old days and he had grown up a bit – not a lot, but a bit.

Chapter 8

MANAGERS

THE MAN IN THE PINK JAGUAR

I KNEW Graham Taylor was England management material when he arrived at Lincoln City as a 23-year-old in 1968. He struck me then as a very serious young man who knew where he was going and knew what he wanted to achieve in the game. But the main thing about Graham is that, despite his strong links with the Football Association which has made him England boss, he is very much his own man and will do things his way.

That season we spent together as players, Lincoln were going for promotion but suffered a bad dip in form. The manager, Ron Gray, called a team meeting out in the middle of the pitch one day to try and sort out what was going wrong. He had his say and then asked if the players had anything to add and young Graham pointed his finger at three players and said: 'He's not working hard enough; he's not doing it; and he's not.' I have not seen many people with the bottle to do that, but it showed his courage and conviction.

Taylor was always management potential – a very well organised person and a man of the establishment. He spent a lot of his spare time coaching and when I went to do my full FA coach's badge, Graham was one of the examiners – and he's four years younger than me!

Whether he can make a success of the England job remains to be seen, but I believe he has the capability. What he will also need is his share of luck.

We have just gone through an era where standards have fallen significantly in the English game and we have produced very few top-class players. However, there are signs that things are improving and the last World Cup in Italy certainly showed that other countries' standards are not that high. So maybe Graham Taylor will have the little bit of luck that sees him taking charge at a time when we have a few world-class players coming through. He definitely has a chance with the likes of Paul Gascoigne, Paul Parker, Des Walker and Mark Wright – though I'm not totally convinced about Taylor's Villa old boy David Platt.

However, despite Graham's qualities, he would not have been my first choice to succeed Bobby Robson. I favoured my old pal Howard Kendall.

Howard has won League Championships, won in Europe and managed abroad at Bilbao. No disrespect to Graham, but Kendall is the more complete manager. But I suspect Howard knew the England job was cut-and-dried for Taylor and that's why he did not let himself be put forward for it after Robson quit.

Howard and I used to socialise together. We would have some heavy sessions after a hard day's coaching and Howard would see us all off and still be fresh as a daisy next day. He also has a great passion for Chinese food. I always remember him taking me out for a big Chinese meal before QPR's League Cup semi-final against Liverpool – something I wasn't sure was such a good idea. But we got the result which took us to Wembley and Howard rang me afterwards and said: 'Always have a Chinese before an important game!'

Howard is a very strong man as a manager, but he is more of a coach/manager and I think that is why he did so well at Bilbao where he didn't have to deal with contracts but could concentrate on the football. There is a lot to be said for that Continental system of running a team. In England, managers get bogged down by transfer deals and financial negotiations and it interferes with their work with the team. Abroad they let a general manager sort out transfers and players' contracts, so the team boss can give 100 per cent to the football side.

Malcolm Allison was another man who probably worked

Graham Taylor . . . showed his qualities at Lincoln City

better with that system, as his success in Portugal indicated. He would not want to spend hours trying to do a deal with a player – his attitude was more 'I want him, so how much will it cost? . . . right, there it is.' That's why he probably needed a restraining hand on him financially.

Bobby Robson is in Holland now enjoying the Continental system, decent wages and being out of the firing line of the English Press. When I went into League management in 1972, Bobby was one of the first bosses I met. I was in the Fourth Division with Colchester United and he was in charge at Ipswich Town in the First. We lived about 12 miles apart and he used to give me lifts to Lilleshall for managers' meetings. He also gave an insight into the pressures of running a club in the top flight.

Robson had been sacked by Fulham and was having a bad time at Ipswich. Results were not going well and the fans were giving him a lot of stick. The chants of 'Robson out!' had started up and Bobby feared he was for the boot again. There was an Ipswich board meeting the day after a bad defeat which had sparked more aggro from the supporters and Bobby felt he was in trouble. But the chairman, Patrick Cobbold, stood up right at the start of the meeting and said: 'First of all, I would like to apologise to our manager for the disgraceful behaviour of some of our fans.'

I have never heard of anything like that happening before, but that was Ipswich Town. The secret of their success was continuity and that's a rare thing in football – they got their reward when Bobby eventually developed a tremendous team for them.

Even in those days, Robson struck me as a top manager. He had authority and he had something else that impressed me – a brand new Jaguar! I thought it was absolutely magnificent, but it was coloured pink and all Bobby did was moan about the colour. Personally, I would have been happy to have the car in any colour, but within a few days Bobby had swapped it for a different colour. That is when I knew what it took to be a First Division manager . . . a man who could complain about a brand new Jag.

Bobby, of course, went on to become England boss and the

Howard Kendall . . . my choice for England manager

target for the most over-the-top campaign of vilification I have ever seen. I thought Robson was a good choice for the job and, overall, he did well. Plus, it should be remembered that he held the reins at a time when we had the fewest true international-class players of any era. Bobby could only do the job with the players at his disposal and the harsh truth is that many of them were not good enough.

111

His biggest disappointment was the 1988 European Championships in Germany when England lost all three group matches. But if Gary Lineker had been on his usual striking form, we would have beaten both the Republic of Ireland and Holland. While some of the criticism which followed was justified, much of it was ridiculous and out of all proportion. Still, the bigger you are, the more stick you get.

Our hopes were high going into the last World Cup, but after the draw with Ireland Bobby took another hammering. Yet, it was exactly the sort of game most of us would have expected to see. The team grew in confidence and had a good tournament, and I was pleased for Robson that he came out of it with credit after the way he had been treated by the media. He had his bit of luck in stumbling on to the sweeper system. I am sure that he had not planned that for the later stages – it was forced on him – but he deserved the break.

While England got a real boost from the World Cup, the game in general did not. As far as new ideas went, it was a non-event. Innovation in tactics and in dead-ball situations was conspicuous by its absence and the overall level of performance was very ordinary – even the Germans got worse as they went on.

The biggest spoiler for England was the furore over Robson's new job with PSV Eindhoven which broke just before the squad departed for Italy. Quite simply, the FA had told him they were not going to renew his contract and he wanted to keep working, so he was perfectly entitled to listen to offers.

His big mistake – and his only mistake – was not announcing that he had accepted the Eindhoven job immediately. He should have done what Germany's Franz Beckenbauer and Argentina's Carlos Bilardo did and come clean that he was quitting. In soccer you cannot keep a £1,000-transfer quiet, never mind the England manager going off to Holland.

I appreciate what he was trying to do – get the squad away to Sardinia and then make the announcement. But these things always come out and it looked very messy. However, people calling him a traitor when, in effect, he had got the sack and taken another job, is ludicrous. There is no logic in that kind of attack.

I was in Rome in July for the World Cup final and I bumped

into Bobby there. Being a die-hard Newcastle United fan, he commiserated with me over our missing out on promotion. His parting shot was: 'I'll see you in two years, Jim, I'm off to earn some real money now.'

I responded: 'You're a traitor, Bob' and we had a laugh.

But he was right – the England job is not well paid. It is worth about £100,000 a year and you make a bit on the side through endorsements etc, but you should not need to be picking up cash from endorsements as England's manager. If you look at what he went through and the responsibility he carried over eight years – and eight years as a national manager is like 16 at club level – he was paid peanuts. His wages were far out-stripped by other international managers.

I was once asked if I had ever fancied the England manager's job, but while it is one ambition of every player to play for his country – and I regret that I never made it – managing my country does not have that much appeal. I prefer the day-to-day business of dealing with players and running a club.

In any case, I have never been part of the FA establishment. Whenever I have gone to Lilleshall, it has been to enjoy and educate myself rather than meet the right people and shake the right hands.

But another of the men linked with the England job was Howard Wilkinson and I can claim some small credit for setting him on his management career.

Howard, a winger with two good feet, was given a free transfer by Brighton. While he could have stayed in the League, he wanted to train to be a teacher, so I signed him for Boston United as a part-time pro and he split his time between Boston and teacher-training college. Funnily enough, Howard has become known for his long-ball tactics, but I always recall him as a winger who wanted the ball played to his feet. It is often the case that players change when they become managers. Howard was a bit of a hurdler as a winger, but now he demands tremendous physical presence from his team.

He was an intelligent lad and when I left Boston I recom-mended him to chairman Ernest Malkinson as my replacement. Malkinson thought Howard was too young and, instead, made him coach with Keith Jobling as manager. But Howard soon got the top job at Boston and enjoyed great success before going on to Notts County, Sheffield Wednesday and Leeds – as well as England Under–21s.

Howard was one of the first managers to work scientifically on fitness training and I'm sure he will continue to do well. I know he feels stung by the tag of long-ball merchant which has stuck to him, because he has always had more to offer and I think we will see him develop the game at Leeds.

One of my biggest friends in management is Ron Atkinson.

He has picked up this reputation for being flamboyant, wearing lots of jewellery and drinking champagne. But, basically, that is all a load of rubbish. It is an image – and maybe one that he doesn't mind too much – but it is seriously over-done. Ron certainly used to buy champagne, but he rarely drank it . . . he just used to top me up. And I feel that this image has often obscured what a good manager he is.

Sure, Big Ron likes the limelight. But underneath he is a real football man with a top-class knowledge of the game. He created a good side at West Brom and another at Manchester United, where he was very hard done by when he got the sack. He had personal problems at the time with his marriage breaking up and when that was splashed in the newspapers it gave Manchester United the opportunity to get rid of him. I spoke to him just before he got the elbow and he was on the point of resigning anyway – he felt he had lost it with the players.

I had got to know United's chairman Martin Edwards through Ron, and when Oxford had a series of League Cup ties against Man United in 1984, Martin, Ron, myself and our wives had all gone out for dinner after each match. But I sensed Ron's job was in danger two years later when I went to Southampton to watch United play there. I met Martin Edwards on the stairway and he just said 'Hello' and hurried on. He would normally have chatted and I thought, 'You're in trouble here, Ron.' United also lost the game 4–0, which did nothing to help Ron. He lost his job a couple of days later and, in view of the pressure he was under at home and at work, I wonder if it was not a relief.

I had become chummy with Ron while I was at Birmingham and he took over at West Brom. We had quite a nice circle in

Ron Atkinson . . . in trouble at Manchester United

Birmingham, with Ron, John Barnwell at Wolves, Gordon Milne at Coventry and myself, and all the wives used to get on, too. In fact, the only non-socialiser was Ron Saunders at Aston Villa.

Big Ron, Gordon and I used to go on holiday together and there was one time in Marbella when we had a footballers' 'Who's Who?' together for a barbecue. The occasion was my daughter Suzanne's birthday and in attendance were Kenny Dalglish, Frank Gray, Jock Wallace, Gordon Milne, Ron Atkinson, Tony Book, Ron Wylie and Liverpool physio Roy Evans. Not a bad impromptu turn-out. Dalglish was much as he is now – a closed book. He is just not the sort of guy you get to know well and, in any case, I always had trouble with his accent.

While I have never consciously followed another manager's style, I am sure that I picked things up from all the managers I played under and a lot of things I learnt in those early days have stood me in good stead.

My first manager was Joe Mercer at Sheffield United, a man with great enthusiasm and a real love for the game. Joe had a different suit on every time I saw him and he was always immaculate in collar and tie. That struck me very strongly and brought home the need for players and club officials to look smart and present the right image. When a team arrives at a game in matching club blazers or suits, you always feel they have something about them and that they are prepared.

In my playing days, one of the first things you did as a youngster was go out and buy a tailored suit with your signing-on fee. That was what separated the player from the rest of his mates – the player had the money to buy a nice suit. Joe Mercer used to play with THE Arsenal and they used to say that when you joined THE Arsenal, the first thing they bought you was an evening suit.

Though I have served a long stint as a Football League manager, there is one man who has been in the business even longer – the one and only Brian Clough. Of course, I had lengthy dealings with Cloughie when I sold Trevor Francis from Birmingham to Nottingham Forest in 1979, but while I got an insight into his style I got no clues as to the reasons for his longevity or success. The fact is that wherever you go with football people – and especially managers – Brian Clough will be discussed. And it is usually along the lines of 'How the hell does he do it?' because we hear the stories that he does not spend much time at the ground; that he does not take the training etc.

The truth is that no one knows his secret.

I asked Archie Gemmill when I had him at Birmingham and his answer was: 'Small wages and large bonuses.' Trevor Francis emphasised the fear factor. He told me that Clough's number two, Peter Taylor, was like a teacher at school. But when Cloughie arrived it was like the headmaster walking in.

I certainly had the chance to witness first hand Brian's unique way of handling players when I was invited as a guest to the European Cup final between Nottingham Forest and Hamburg in 1980. And my verdict on Cloughie's behaviour at that auspicious occasion was 'plain crazy'.

I suspect the invitation came because I had sold them Francis and he had repaid the investment by scoring the only goal against Malmo which took the European Cup to Forest the year before. Anyway, the 1980 final was in Madrid and Derby County official Stuart Webb, who had a travel firm, was organising the trip. My wife Yvonne and I were in an official party that included all the players and staff and their wives – plus about eight Taylors and ten Cloughs. Brian, Peter and the team were in a hotel in the mountains, while the rest of us stopped at a super hotel in Madrid.

An official banquet was arranged for after the match to which everyone was invited – everyone except the players, that is! For reasons known only to himself, Cloughie decided to ban the players from the banquet regardless of the result. And the rest of us were told to keep quiet so that the players and their wives did not find out.

I thought the whole thing was daft, but assumed Clough would have a change of heart, especially when Forest retained the Cup against a Kevin Keegan-led Hamburg with John Robertson getting the winner. But there was no shifting Clough. So we went back to the hotel, got changed and made our way to the banquet – and there were all the players wives in their evening frocks sitting around a table waiting for their victorious menfolk to turn up. That team included the likes of Peter Shilton, Viv Anderson, Larry Lloyd, Kenny Burns, Gary Birtles and Ian Bowyer. Poor Stuart Webb had to pluck up the courage to tell the wives that the players had been confined to barracks at their mountain retreat. There was bedlam when the news broke . . . the girls were aghast and many began crying. Even the staff were crying!

About one o'clock in the morning a bunch of players arrived at the banqueting suite – they had broken camp and I don't blame them. I suppose that was the start of the break-up of that great Forest team.

There was no logic to what Cloughie had done, but then he is the sort who likes to defy logic. Still, his record is second to none – just like his methods – and I believe he would have made a very good England manager.

I make the comparison between Clough and Jack Charlton's approach to the Republic of Ireland job. Neither likes to get too involved with the day-to-day business. They would rather concentrate on preparing players for the big games. They are both independent enough to put two fingers up to the world. They can say: 'I'm doing the job my way and if you don't like it, then tough!'

And both are financially secure enough to be able to stand up to their bosses. That's a handy position for a manager to be in.

Chapter 9

CHAIRMEN

EXORCISM AT ST ANDREWS

CLUB CHAIRMEN take a lot of stick these days, but I've been lucky in that my bosses – and they include controversial characters like Robert Maxwell and Jim Gregory – have, by and large, been straight and honest in their dealings with me.

The man who gave me my first job in soccer management was Ernest Malkinson at Boston United and he would have made a great Football League chairman. A wealthy man who chain-smoked cigars, he made his money from the Englishman's passion for gambling. He ran a number of bingo and concert halls and it was this interest that had got him declared *sine die* by the FA some years before my arrival.

Using his knowledge of the bingo scene, he started one of the first ever lotteries at a football club, declaring that lotteries would save soccer from financial ruin. And he was proved right. For a period lotteries did keep many clubs afloat. But it ended up costing him, because he had not got the necessary FA permission when he started his scheme.

It was an immediate success and he had £20,000 in the kitty before the FA moved in, froze the cash and kicked Malkinson out of the game. It was decreed that the £20,000 could not go to Boston United, but had to be used for sporting activities. And so it was used to set up Boston FC, a bone in Malkinson's throat for many years after and the start of a fierce rivalry. Malkinson was let back into the game, but never got over how

119

the cash he had raised for his beloved United had been used to set up opposition on his doorstep.

And I really found out what pressure was all about when we drew Boston FC in the preliminary round of the FA Cup. For us it was like Liverpool v Everton. We were on a bonus for every goal we scored. By the time we were 4–0 up, the chairman was shouting 'Offside!' every time we attacked!

Ernest Malkinson died almost immediately after watching the 1986 League Cup final when I led Queen's Park Rangers out at Wembley against Oxford. He had been very ill and his wife always said he was determined to hang on to see me take a team to Wembley.

Roy Chapman, chairman at Colchester, was also a super bloke but a little too nice for the job. Colchester had a big board and he wanted to be very democratic and give everyone a say. The job was taking too much of his time and he quit due to family pressure. He was replaced by Robert Jackson, who is still my personal solicitor and a good friend.

At Blackburn I was under Bill Bancroft, now an FA councillor. He was a very smart man and believed his club should be the same. The entrance to Rovers, the directors' box and the guest room were all top class and that was down to him. And he also put tradition before a quick profit. For when all the shirt manufacturers were first coming in and suggesting a change of strip to make some money, he refused to alter the famous blue-and-white halves that symbolised Blackburn Rovers. I admire him tremendously for that.

But he was also a character and I've seen him drop his trousers and stand on the bar and sing when he's had a few drinks.

He would always wish us all the best before the game and – win, lose or draw – he was the first one at the dressing-room after the game to shake all the lads' hands. In fact, he was usually there with the cigarettes out . . . for which our winger Dave Wagstaffe was particularly grateful.

When we had a long away trip and climbed on board the coach on a Friday, Bancroft would put his arm round me and say: 'Well Jim, you've done your work – now you're on holiday!'

When I joined Birmingham I stayed that first night at the

home of chairman Keith Coombs, arriving in darkness. Next morning I went down and said: 'What a lovely house – and what a fabulous view of the park.' Of course, it wasn't the park . . . it was his gardens.

Coombs was a keen reader of the *Rothman's Football Year-book* – it was his Bible – and that was how he chose me as manager. He worked out that I'd improved the points total each season of every team I had been with.

Keith was a lovely chap – even though he sacked me. His father, Clifford Coombs, had made Birmingham very successful and Keith wanted to emulate him, but never succeeded. Even though I was his choice, I believe that he was persuaded the day Ron Saunders quit Aston Villa after taking them to the Championship that Saunders was the man to lead Birmingham into Europe. That was the gloryland he was looking for and I think others on the board put pressure on him to get rid of me. I don't know if Ron touted for my job, but he did attend a dinner with our vice-chairman while waiting for a vacancy to occur.

I have some consolation. Keith Coombs has said to me since that replacing me with Ron Saunders was the worst day's work he ever did. I know what he meant – he left the club having lost huge amounts of his own money.

It's strange that a big city like Birmingham has not established itself at the top, but one explanation is the gypsy curse. Many, many years ago, the gypsies cursed the St Andrews ground – at least that's what people told us – and Coombs took it seriously enough to start looking for an exorcist.

He approached the Catholic Church and they wouldn't touch it. He went to the Church of England and they didn't want to know. A few others turned down the job, too.

So we ended up with the Greek Orthodox Church and, to be fair, they had a good stab at it. Their priest turned out in all his robes, complete with holy water and a cross, and went round the dressing-rooms and ground – even the training ground – sprinkling water as he went. I couldn't believe it – they even buried four crosses at each corner of the pitch!

But it still didn't work. Then again, the Greeks have never been much cop at football.

Birmingham City is the only club to have sacked me – so far – but I was only out of work a week. I'd met an Oxford director, Paul Reeves, through Ron Atkinson and when I got the bullet he recommended me to Oxford chairman Robert Maxwell. An interview was fixed up for the night I was due to fly out on holiday with my family to a villa in Majorca which Doug Ellis of Aston Villa had kindly loaned me.

The meeting was at Maxwell's Pergamon Press office in Oxford, but he had to break off for another meeting at his home 50 yards away. He told me to wait an hour and have a drink and a sandwich, so I had to tell him I was due to fly from Manchester and my wife and kids were waiting for me at home. He said he would organise all the flights and tickets for me to travel the following day and then phoned my wife.

'Jimmy's tied up,' he told her. 'Do you want to go to Majorca on your own or wait and go with him tomorrow?'

So he took over our holiday arrangements and we went the next day.

That gave me an early idea of Maxwell's power and ability to get things done. He was so impressive as a man and I knew he had the strength of character and financial clout to help me do something with Oxford. If we'd ever got into Europe, he would have been useful. He speaks nine languages and I've often been in his office while he's taken calls and switched fluently from one language to another.

I remember turning up at his house smoking a small cigar and he made me put it out, insisting I have one of his. He handed me a huge Havana which I could hardly hold up.

One half-time I was having a go at the players and out of the corner of my eye I saw this figure in a blue coat enter the dressing-room. I thought it was one of the fans, which is the sort of thing that could happen at Oxford.

I finished my spiel and turned round to turf the guy out and it was Maxwell, sitting there with a cup of tea and smiling benignly. He told me later that he'd wanted to see me at work and he even came in the dug-out with me once. But he only lasted ten minutes before all the cursing and swearing got to him.

Still, if I wanted a player and agreed a fee – like £70,000 for John Aldridge from Newport – Maxwell would go 'bang' and

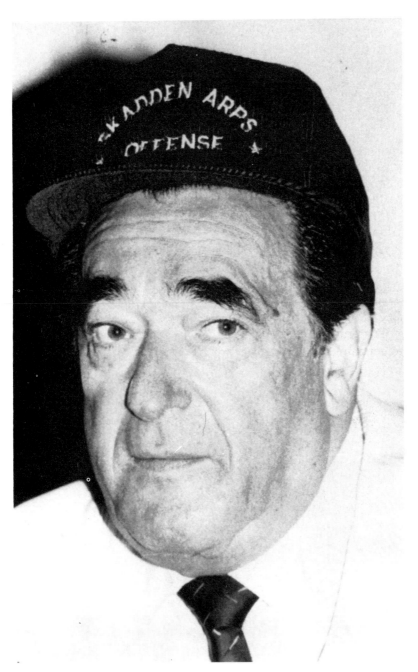

Robert Maxwell . . . the all-powerful chairman at Oxford United

there would be the money on its way to the other club. They couldn't believe they could get it all at one go and were delighted. That was very important in us beating other clubs to players.

Oxford were pushing for the Third Division title in 1984 when I got a call from the chairman one day. 'Oxford and Reading are joining together and you are the new manager of Thames Valley Royals,' he told me. He'd done a deal to buy Reading and was planning to amalgamate the clubs with me in charge and Reading's manager Maurice Evans as my assistant.

I'd not been consulted, but I was happy still to be in a job and so it was OK by me. Unfortunately, the fans were dead against it and I took a lot of stick from them over it. I was very much the piggy-in-the-middle and I understood the feelings of the supporters of both clubs.

The fans' resistance was fierce and in one game against Wigan those in front of the directors' box never watched a bit of football. They just showered the chairman with abuse and spit. They couldn't reach me – I sat too far back in the box – and the visiting directors all moved back as well. But Bob Maxwell just sat at the front and took the whole brunt . . . he was a brave bastard.

The deal fell through because the people at the Reading end couldn't deliver, but I'm convinced Maxwell would have ploughed on with it given the chance. And it also showed up a little known caring side to the newspaper magnate. For Roger Smee won the battle to take control of Reading and he sacked Maurice Evans who had been supportive of the merger. The following season when I needed a chief scout, I suggested Evans to the chairman.

'Done,' said Maxwell. 'He's a good man, I'll phone him now.'

I was left scratching my head – 'How does Maxwell have Maurice's phone number?'

It transpired that when Maurice had got the sack Maxwell had phoned him straight away and offered him financial help to tide him over till he got another job. That gesture simply amazed me.

But it wasn't all plain sailing. Maxwell wasn't that interested in the football and the day-to-day side of the club, but he wanted to be a winner and get the publicity that went with success. When I took Oxford from the Third to the Second Division, I went to a meeting with him and our contractual discussion lasted only ten minutes before all was agreed.

The following season we went up to the First Division, but on the day we played at Leeds needing a win for the title, he came out with his hobby horse about us quitting the Manor Ground and moving to the purpose-built stadium. I was asked to appear on Saturday lunchtime's *Saint & Greavsie* show before the Leeds match and, with no warning, the first question was: 'Your chairman has just been on national news to say that Oxford will not play at the Manor Ground next season. What do you say?'

I said: 'Well, Mr Maxwell is a very capable chairman, but I'm convinced we will be at the Manor Ground next year.'

At 2.05 p.m. I got a call at Elland Road from you-know-who – 'So you're going to pay the players' wages next year, are you? You have just gone on television against your chairman saying we will play at the Manor Ground.'

My point was that if he'd told me he was going to come out with this plan, I would have been better prepared to deal with the question. But he wasn't having it and the argument raged on. It was by now 2.20 p.m. and an important promotion game was pressing, so I ended up by telling him to stuff the job up his backside and slammed the phone down!

That was the start of our relationship going on to the rocks.

Two days later I was in another meeting with him and told him I'd done a deal with Adidas who would provide strips for the club from first team down to youth team – boots, training gear, balls and about £10,000 cash. It was a great deal for us. But he gave me such stick over it, saying things like Liverpool got £200,000 for their kit deal. I pointed out that Liverpool sold about a million replicas while Oxford sold about ten, but it cut no ice with Maxwell and he said he'd get us a better deal.

He came back with an Umbro deal worth £20,000 – 'Kit, boots and balls,' he said.

'But Umbro don't make boots and balls.'

'Oh, well, you'll have to go to Adidas for boots and balls.'

I patiently explained that we couldn't go back to Adidas having turned them down and then done a deal with their rivals. We ended up with a worse deal and it showed that his little bit of knowledge could be dangerous.

A week later we were Second Division champions and I was looking for a better contract, but he was a hard man to pin down. I finally got him in his office and gave my figure. He said 'No' and we started to negotiate but were interrupted – not for the first time – and the meeting was never concluded.

Two weeks later we had another go, but there were more interruptions as he was dragged away by phone calls and various other meetings. He eventually came back and said 'Well, you're not happy with what I give you, so you can speak to anyone you want.'

To this day I don't know if he wanted me to stay at Oxford or to leave. Maybe I was a bit hasty, but things had broken down a bit between us and I went to see Jim Gregory and joined Queen's Park Rangers.

However, that was not the end of my dealings with Captain Bob, for two years later, when the Oxford job was vacant again, he asked to see me, having heard that I wasn't too happy at QPR.

It was at his home on a lovely day and he came out of a business meeting with no shoes on and suggested we strolled round the garden. We ended up talking while lying stretched out on the grass.

I'd decided that I wanted to be well looked after and that if the deal was good enough I'd stay at Oxford for keeps. But he asked me how long was left on my contract and when I told him one year he said it might be better if I saw my contract out and then came back to Oxford. It was then I realised I'd just wasted my afternoon. I don't know what had happened, but he had clearly changed his mind from the morning when he rang and seemed set to offer me the job.

So it was back to Jim Gregory, a complex man who could be as nice as pie one day and a nightmare the next.

Jim had a good knowledge of the game and that could be a bit of a problem. If I wanted to buy a defender, instead of being able to say who I wanted, I had to put up four names.

Sometimes I got the one I wanted, but sometimes we ended up buying the one Jim Gregory wanted.

His argument was that it was his money and he was right. And he had done a tremendous job building up QPR. But Jim was a frustrated football manager, although he would always support you when needed. But it made him rather intimidating to work for and there was always pressure to bend to his will.

I recall one deal I tried to set up to bring Irish international Ray Houghton from Fulham to Loftus Road for £125,000. Jim Gregory wouldn't pay the money and there was definitely a personality battle going on between him and Fulham's chairman Ernie Clay over who would give way first. The longer it dragged on, the worse it got. It was my first signing and already it was beginning to look like a pressure signing because, if I got Houghton for the money, he was going to have to score three goals every game to satisfy the chairman. So when I got a call from Gregory saying he'd got me Houghton, I said I didn't want him. I cut my nose off to spite my face.

But Jim could also be a lot of fun and he loved being one of the lads with the players, something he missed as he got older. He was also a wheeler-dealer who loved the buying and selling of players – and he was good at it.

We were in a restaurant once when there was a call for him and it was Chelsea's Ken Bates who wanted to know how much we wanted for centre-half Steve Wicks. Jim turned to me and I said: '£250,000 . . . £300,000 would be great if we can get it.' So he picks up the phone: '£500,000 – please yourself, ring me back in ten minutes if you want him.'

I thought no way is this deal coming off, but ten minutes later Bates was on the phone. '£475,000 – done!' said a delighted Jim. 'But you've got to sign him by seven o'clock tonight or it's off.'

He then turned to me and said: 'You, you're some manager . . . you'd have taken £250,000.'

There was still a problem, because though Steve wanted away he had always said he would not go to Chelsea. So Gregory told me to tell him that a big club had been in for him, but we'd turned it down because it was Chelsea. Steve insisted he was interested, so I sent him along to see Ken Bates with the warning he had to sign there and then or the deal was off. That was Jim's way of making sure Steve Wicks signed.

But Jim's biggest sale was the club itself. He flogged it for £6 million in February 1987 to David Bulstrode and Marler Estates, who owned Fulham's Craven Cottage and Chelsea's Stamford Bridge. I was amazed he was prepared to let it go after he'd done so much, but again perhaps it was that wheeler-dealer instinct.

I was naturally apprehensive about David Bulstrode taking over because new chairmen have their own ideas and, sometimes, have their own managers lined up. But we got on very well. As an ex-bank manager and a person of some refinement, he was the opposite to Gregory. He was very ambitious for the game and quickly got on to the Football League Management Committee. In fact, if he hadn't died, I'm convinced he would have become the President of the Football League.

He took the Omniturf up after one year at Loftus Road. Jim Gregory had done it to give the team the edge and get them in the First Division and keep them there. It had cost £350,000 in 1981 – the League's first artificial pitch – and had certainly done its job. But Bulstrode preferred grass and so did I. To be fair, so did Jim Gregory and I believe he intended to revert back to grass if he had stayed at QPR.

Marler got a lot of criticism because people just regarded them as property speculators and thought they were going to close clubs down, but Bulstrode was a football nut and had big plans for QPR. They included putting a sliding roof over the ground. However, he died completely out of the blue in September 1988, aged just 47.

Richard Thompson, another Marler director, came in – the most unusual chairman I've ever had because he was just 22 years old. Thompson took over because his father had bought heavily into Marler and, while we got on, it was very strange. It was like talking to my son – it just didn't feel right.

Sheffield Wednesday inquired about me, but they wouldn't let me speak to them. Yet they said OK when Newcastle came in. They weren't desperate to hang on to me . . . perhaps I was a bit long in the tooth and old-fashioned for their tastes and

With chairman Gordon McKeag at Newcastle

there was Trevor Francis on hand who probably suited their image more.

And that brings me to my current chairman, Gordon McKeag.

I got a good vibe from him when I spoke to him about the job, but I had no idea of the personal hell he was going through at the club over the threatened takeover. A campaign was being waged against the board and McKeag was the subject of much scorn and abuse from the supporters. Yet he was extremely brave and courageous – almost to the point of silliness – over handling the flak. He was receiving obscene phone calls and I said he should go ex-directory but, typical of the man, he said he and his wife had had the same phone number all their married life and they were not going to change it now. I know what I would have done in his shoes, but I could not help but be impressed with the way he conducted himself.

McKeag has many good qualities and is a tremendous sports enthusiast. When we went on a pre-season tour, I nicknamed him Action Man . . . he was cycling in the morning, running in the afternoon and playing tennis in the evening. But the biggest thing about him is that he is Newcastle United daft. And it was quite upsetting that when the anti-board campaign was at its peak his opponents suggested that because he spoke properly he was not a football fan. That slant, that he has no great love for the club or the game, is totally wrong and totally unfair.

Gordon works practically full-time at Newcastle, but he is also on the Football League Management Committee and FA committees. I'm not sure that is for the best with a big club like Newcastle because his League and FA business is very time-consuming. People might think that it is of benefit to United to have a man in such a powerful position, but it doesn't always work that way. Some chairmen go into those positions with a vested interest and will look after their own clubs, but not Gordon McKeag. When he's sitting on committees, his job is to do what is right for English football, rather than what is right for Newcastle United FC. But I welcome that approach because we have to look beyond the interests of our own clubs and concentrate on the betterment of the game.

There is too much self-interest on these committees and I think that is reflected in the decision to promote Sunderland to the First Division at the end of the 1989–90 season after Swindon had been demoted for financial irregularities. The League could have promoted Newcastle or not relegated Sheffield Wednesday to fill the vacant spot in Division One. But either of those decisions would have destroyed the play-offs and the play-offs are very important to a lot of chairmen and their clubs. They mean extra money for small clubs because the gate money is shared round the rest of the division. Newcastle lost money competing in the play-offs, but a lot of clubs made money off our back. The play-offs were created for mediocrity, but the League needed to give them credibility. That's self-interest at committee level.

And that's why we need more people in the upper levels of the game who are prepared to make the right decision, whether it hurts their club or not. Gordon McKeag is that sort of person.

I know that he rubs people up the wrong way sometimes. He is a solicitor and that is how he comes over – well-spoken, precise, forceful – and often what he says goes over the top of people's heads. He lacks the common touch, but he can be extremely witty and he is a throwback to some of my earlier chairmen with an old-fashioned style of doing business.

With the Maxwells, Gregorys and Bulstrodes, you have the entrepreneurs, the wheeler-dealer chairmen. You deal with them on a one-to-one basis and they call the shots. At Newcastle it is back to the old style with board meetings, discussion and debate and then a vote, with the majority decision holding sway.

The problem with board meetings, in my experience, is that they go on for a long time and they don't make too many decisions. There's a tendency to try and keep everyone happy and often the manager doesn't get what he wants, which is a 'Yes' or 'No'. A board can spend two weeks making a decision that I need in two minutes. So it is probably best from a manager's point of view to have an all-powerful chairman and just deal with one man.

Of course, the key thing is your relationship with that one man. If that's not right, then you don't stay together very long.

Chapter 10

THE CHANGING FACE OF THE GAME

HEROES AND VILLAINS

RON ATKINSON first gave me the name 'The Bald Eagle'.
He's a mate, but I am not sure I should thank him for that. I
was in charge at Birmingham at the time and he was bossing
West Brom. We were flying high and bidding for promotion
when Ron did a piece in a newspaper dubbing me 'The Bald
Eagle' – for better or worse, it stuck!

I have had less flattering titles. When I took the Birmingham
job, the headline in the local paper was 'Jimmy Who?' Fair
enough, I had moved there from Blackburn and was scarcely
a big name. I suppose that headline reflected the fact that I had
done it the hard way, climbing from the bottom rung by rung.
In an ideal world, my progression would have followed a
different route.

It has always been a regret that I have never been anything
other than a manager and I have no doubt that the best way to
start is to go as number two at a very good club – preferably in
the First Division. That way you would see how a top club is
run – from the administration to the coaching – and, with that
background, you could take over at a club in the lower echelons.
Then again, I have always been opinionated and wanted to
make decisions, so it is debatable how good a number two I
would have made.

I never earned the kind of money top players got, so I have
never felt financially secure and have always been looking over

my shoulder worrying about getting the sack because I have had a mortgage to pay and mouths to feed. That makes a manager's life doubly difficult. In any case, the job has become a lot harder now – clubs demand instant success, while players are more interested in money and consequently less loyal. That is why I have a lot of sympathy for any young manager coming into the game.

A lot of clubs struggle along on a shoestring. The manager has to sell his best players to keep the club afloat and, when results go badly, he gets the chop.

People come into management and then disappear without trace. Somehow I have survived – I am 50 now and have had 18 years as a Football League boss. What is the secret of longevity in such a difficult occupation?

Well, being fairly successful has helped me out-last most, but my success is based on two main ingredients . . . hard graft and commonsense.

It becomes very demanding when you have to travel to five matches in a week and then when you go home the job is still on your mind. Yes, there are flashes of brilliance and there is always that element of luck, but successful management in my book is 95 per cent perspiration, five per cent inspiration.

I have never been one to plan my career and I don't know how many more years I will want under the kind of pressure that is part and parcel of the craving for soccer glory. I certainly will not hang about in a job just for the sake of it. I still want the buzz of running a big club and when that buzz goes, I will be heading out the door, too.

A number of managerial careers have revolved around part-nerships – Brian Clough and Peter Taylor, Joe Mercer and Malcolm Allison are the most striking examples. I have never had a regular number two because I don't believe in sacking people when I go to a new club. If they cannot do the job then, fair enough, they will be on their way, but when I move in somewhere I think it is right to give the existing staff the chance to prove themselves.

Bobby Roberts, who was with me at Colchester, is one man I would have taken with me. But when I got the Blackburn job, he took the chance to become the gaffer at Colchester.

My current assistant, Bobby Saxton, is a long-time friend. When Blackburn were looking for a new manager, the chairman rang me and suggested Bob – I said he would be an excellent choice and I was proved right.

Bobby and I have plenty of arguments because we feel so deeply about what we are doing and take defeat so badly. But just because we argue does not mean we have fallen out. I know I would sooner have a number two who argues with me than one who agrees with me all the time.

While I have played for four clubs and managed seven others, I did neither with the club that will always have a special place in my heart – my home-town favourites, Sheffield Wednesday. However, I did create a little piece of history at Hillsborough. In April 1986, I took QPR to play Wednesday and thus chalked up the distinction of having managed teams at all 92 League grounds. I got a nice plaque and photo to mark the occasion.

I was actually invited to apply for the Wednesday job a few years ago, but I could foresee problems. Going to a city where all your family and friends are creates extra pressure and the job is difficult enough. Howard Wilkinson was appointed and did very well. Later on, when I felt experienced enough to handle things at Hillsborough, Wednesday came in for me, but QPR would not let them talk to me.

When I watched Wednesday as a lad, anyone who played in the blue-and-white stripes was my idol. In those days you supported the team and would never say a Sheffield Wednesday player was no good. But the nature of support has been changed quite markedly by the media. I recall the days of supporters – now we have critics.

The instinct of the press and TV is to knock players and clubs, rather than build them up. The media is awash with experts who all have a point of view which they peddle to their audience.

At Newcastle United, everyone from the directors to the office staff to the fans is so critical and 'knowledgeable'. When I took the job, Jimmy Armfield warned me it would be tricky. He told me: 'The biggest problem is that you have 30,000 internationals watching you.' What this produces is a heroes and villains attitude . . . the heroes can do no wrong and the villains can do no right. It is black and white, yet football is really full of grey areas. Supporters are inclined to consider the individual performance, rather than the team play. It is a case of 'he's bad' and 'he's good'.

Liverpool are probably the only club to have truly educated their fans to appreciate team play as opposed to the individuals in the team. I remember watching Sheffield Wednesday lose 6–5 to West Brom many years ago and all we talked about was what a fantastic match it had been. Then the prizes were not so great and winning was not the be-all and end-all – how you played mattered! And, of course, because there was not the same pressure to get results as today, players could express themselves without fear or inhibition.

It is much harder to be a skilled footballer now. The game is faster, the players fitter, the marking tighter and defenders are more organised with tactics designed to deny the opposition's ability. In that sense, standards are higher than they have ever been. Teams will spend time on tactics to stop people playing rather than say: 'We'll play you and you play us and may the best team win!'

Because of the shortage of quality players and the increasingly well-organised defences, the long-ball game has developed in Britain with teams like Watford and Wimbledon playing the percentages on set pieces and offsides. It has had some success, but that kind of soccer will never, ever bring in the fans, regardless of how successful it is. And perhaps now the wheel is turning again because we are slowly learning that you can beat the long-ball game with superior football skill.

For a manager in the modern era, winning is everything, but I believe that the better your team becomes at playing the game properly, the more success you will have. If you get your side playing good football and passing the ball, you will get the right results in the end.

That may seem a naïve philosophy, but I stick with it. And I am not prepared to try and win at all costs – for example, I would never shorten or narrow a pitch just so we could hoof the ball into our opponents' box from anywhere on the park.

Unfortunately, some of the spectators now do seem to adopt a win-at-all-costs approach. A bloke came up to me at

Birmingham City after we had lost to Stoke and said he could not stand us playing so well and going down. 'I would rather you played crap and won with a dodgy penalty,' was his attitude. We all want to win and there are times when you will be happy for that kind of result, but it would be unacceptable to me to 'play crap and win with a dodgy penalty' every week. You have to learn to live with the fans' passions, but you also have to educate them a bit.

After Newcastle had been hammered by Steve Bull and Wolves at St James's Park, one lad tried to have a go at me in the dug-out and when we lost a vital promotion game against Bradford a small group were spitting and throwing things at us at a time when they should have been trying to lift us for the next match.

There are also increasing problems with players because they have become more and more selfish. For too many of them, it is all about money and not about playing football. The lack of quality means that good players in the less successful teams will inevitably move on, but usually it is the financial aspects that will dictate those moves. They will maintain that they are leaving a club to win medals, but plenty move on and never get a medal.

Loyalty is a thing of the past and that is a shame when you think of a character like Ken Fish who gave 21 years' service to Port Vale and then 21 years to Oxford. When I arrived at the Manor Ground, Ken was well into his 60s and was still juggling the roles of physio, kitman and father confessor to the young kids. The great thing was he had such discipline over the apprentices – they all had to call him 'Mr Fish' and senior players like Kevin Brock and Andy Thomas who were with him years ago still call him 'Mr Fish' whenever they meet him.

When Oxford stopped at a hotel for an away game and the waiters started serving the directors first, he would get up and tell them to stop: 'You don't serve the directors first, you serve the players first,' he would tell them. And if the food was late, he would be in the kitchen giving them a rollicking.

Nowadays, players have less professional pride in their per-formances and too much interest in how much they can make off the pitch. The emphasis on agents and deals has sidetracked them from their main job, which is becoming better at the game which earns them their living in the first place. And yet, in recent years, criticism of the game has often been aimed at managers and coaches and the myth developed that English soccer had gone backwards because we were stifling flair.

The notion that creative players were being over-coached and not being allowed to express themselves became a popular bandwagon to jump on. Then, of course, when we did badly at international level, the cry came up that our coaching was not good enough and we were technically behind the Continentals. It shows that the pundits will twist things to suit their opinions.

I don't believe that any coach worth his salt stifles flair. You encourage players to do their tricks and show their skills, but you make sure they do it in the correct areas of the pitch. You will never over-coach top-class players. But what you have to do is give them an organised framework in which to display their talents.

The coaching thing was an easy peg on which to hang the demise of our game, but not enough responsibility is put on to the players themselves. The long-ball game was born out of the fact that there were not sufficient decent players around who could pass the ball properly.

Another Aunt Sally in recent years has been television, but used correctly it is a great vehicle for the game. If you want to sell soap powder, you advertise it on TV and your sales increase. It is the same when it comes to selling soccer – TV is the best medium.

Live matches have been reintroduced on to the screen and gates are going up – that is not an apparent contradiction, it is a clear connection. But there is a downside to television coverage – you can saturate the public by giving the game too much exposure and it does fuel the increasingly critical perspective. This is especially true with the rerunning of incidents to question a referee's decision. Whatever we may think of refs – and I have had a few run-ins with them – they only have fractions of a second to make up their minds. The camera angles can be used to put any number of interpretations on an incident and referees make an easy target to pick on.

My own interpretations of refs' decisions have landed me in

hot water, but I need to let off steam on the touchline and at times I probably get too embroiled in the game. I sit in the directors' box for the first half when I am calm and objective, limiting myself to kicking the seat in front occasionally – which usually contains a director's wife – and letting the odd word slip out that might upset a director's wife. But when I go down to the dug-out for the second half, it is as though I am playing the game. I still get nervous at matches and all the tension and nervousness builds up and is released from the touchline. It helps get rid of the stress and the odd outburst has probably saved me from a heart attack.

The nerves usually start on Thursday and I may need a few whiskies to sleep on the Friday before a big game. But it shows that the buzz is still there and if you don't get wound up, what is the point of being in the game?

The last time I was before a disciplinary hearing for upsetting an official was after a game at Chelsea when a 'gentleman' called Doug Rougvie elbowed QPR's David Kerslake and splattered his nose all over his face. I started shouting at the ref to do something and the next thing I knew I was being escorted from the touchline by the police. The next day the papers said I was going to physically attack the ref, which was ridiculous.

Another flare-up I lived to regret came when Colchester played Bury in the Third Division and our aggressive centre-half, Stuart Morgan, came up against their centre-forward, Derek Spence, whom I knew would try to get Morgan into trouble.

In the first half Morgan won the ball cleanly from Spence, passed it to Steve Leslie and we romped up the field and scored. The next thing I know, the linesman is flagging over something that happened between Morgan and Spence, the ref sends off Leslie – clearly the wrong man – and the goal is disallowed.

Bobby Smith, the Bury boss, was shouting for the ref to send off one of our guys, so I turned to the Bury trainer, Les Hart, and said: 'If you have to cheat to win games by getting people sent off, it's not worth it.'

Smith then turned on me: 'You leave my trainer alone,' etc, and we had a fair old slanging match. We never got within

20 yards of each other, but again the press had to make the most of it and the papers had us fighting in the tunnel.

Following all the bad publicity, my chairman said I had to ban Stuart Morgan and take the captaincy from him. I managed to get them to stop short of banning him, but Stuart felt the club was not supporting him and he was never the same whole-hearted player for Colchester again. It was a shame because he was a good player who had given a lot to the club.

There have also been the occasional lapses of temper directed at players, though I maintain that my reputation is greatly over-played. In my early days I did fly off the handle a bit and some-times it worked in the sense of getting a good response from the players. I once grabbed John Bailey by the hair – his thick curly hair was just right for that – and lifted him up when I thought he had pulled out of a tackle at Blackburn. I told him if he ever dodged a tackle again he would be out. It gave him a shock and from being a lad with a suspect attitude, he really knuckled down.

But having a go at players can also have a detrimental effect – it can put extra pressure on them which they are not able to handle. It is a strange fact that while the players will often moan about you losing your temper with them, they never remember the times you bought them a drink and said how well they had played.

My philosophy on discipline is to treat the players as adults until they start to behave like children. I am not a stickler for fining them or for time-keeping to the minute – I give them some leeway and hope they respond by showing responsibility. I used to ban beards from my teams, but eventually realised it was a waste of energy because I was just creating a potential problem for myself.

One thing I do now ban is reporters from my office after a game, and that relates to an incident when a private conversa-tion appeared in banner headlines.

Oxford had just beaten Arsenal 3–2 and I had a few reporters back in my office for a drink – among them two senior London pressmen. I said that Arsenal had looked excellent for 30 minutes but, when we got on top, some of their players were missing. I added that players hiding might become a problem for them.

It was said privately and in confidence, but a few days later, on the morning of Arsenal's big game against Manchester United, there it was on the back pages – 'SOUTHERN SOFTIES – Arsenal can't win the Championship!'

By and large I get on well with the Press, but I think the pressure on them to get a story has made them much less professional. The thing that really angers me is when they ring you to check out a story and you deny it and they go ahead and print it. They seem able to write what they want and do not work hard enough to substantiate their stories.

I am not too keen on having the TV cameras behind the scenes either but, in 1988 at Queen's Park Rangers, we had the BBC with us for six weeks while they made a film for their science series *QED*.

The idea was that a sports psychologist would work with the players in an attempt to improve their game through their minds. He worked on relaxing them, getting them to think positively, getting them to take responsibility and to make constructive criticism of their colleagues.

I actually believe there is something in it and he certainly helped a couple of players, Dean Coney and Martin Allen. It was a pity that his stay coincided with us dropping from the top of the table to fifth.

Psychology, of course, plays a big part in the manager's job and I was always fascinated by the way our plastic pitch at Loftus Road could psyche out some teams.

Kenny Dalglish is particularly paranoid about plastic and I wonder if that is why Liverpool rarely get a good result on the surface. He contrasts sharply with one of his predecessors, who turned up at QPR one Friday evening. Tony Ingham, Rangers' commercial manager, was working late in the office and he answered the intercom.

'Joe Fagan here, Liverpool.'

'Bugger off, you little so-and-sos – stop playing with the buzzer,' was Tony's reply.

The buzzer went again: 'Joe Fagan, Liverpool!'

'Alf Ramsey, England!'

When there was a third buzz, Tony decided to investigate and there, indeed, was Joe Fagan and the Liverpool bus outside the ground. They were down in London for a game the next day and, as they were due at Loftus Road in a couple of weeks, they wanted a look at the plastic pitch.

They walked round it, walked on it and walked off. 'Fine, no bother,' said Joe and off they went.

Joe treated it in a matter-of-fact way, while Kenny makes a song and dance about artificial turf and possibly conveys his phobia to his side – though Kenny's team have won at QPR.

Oxford were playing Leeds United in the League Cup at the Manor Ground on a very frosty pitch and Eddie Gray, the Leeds boss, had a look at the surface and said to me: 'We cannot play on this, Jim.'

Straight away I thought: 'That'll do for us', and was determined to get the game played. The ref gave the go-ahead, but half-an-hour before kick-off Eddie was still moaning about the state of the pitch – it must have been worth a goal start.

No matter what you might think of a pitch, you keep it to yourself – otherwise you are just putting doubts into your players' heads. And, in the final analysis, it is the players who make or break you.

I have had hundreds pass through my hands – the great, the good and the plain indifferent – and selecting my best-ever line-up proved an intriguing challenge. So, here goes:

Keeper:	David Seaman (QPR – £200,000 from Birmingham)
Full-Backs:	David Langan (Birmingham and Oxford – £300,000 from Derby; free from Birmingham)
	Mark Dennis (Birmingham and QPR – £20,000 from Southampton)
Central Defenders:	Colin Todd (Birmingham and Oxford – £300,000 from Everton; free from Nottingham Forest)
	Paul Parker (QPR – £200,000 from Fulham)
	Alberto Tarantini (Birmingham – £250,000 from Boca Juniors)

Midfield:	Trevor Hebberd (Oxford – player exchange from Southampton)
	Archie Gemmill (Birmingham – £150,000 from Nottingham Forest)
Forwards:	Trevor Francis (Birmingham and QPR – £25,000 from Rangers)
	John Aldridge (Oxford – £70,000 from Newport County)
	David Wagstaffe (Blackburn – £3,000 from Wolves)

Not a bad side for just over £1 million!

The ideal subs would be Frank Worthington and Kevin Brock and that leaves out an awful lot of quality players. They have given me great delight and not a little heartache, but it has always been interesting. The job is so crazy and defies logic that if you didn't love it, you would not be in it.

CAREER DETAILS

JAMES MICHAEL SMITH

Born: Sheffield on 17 October 1940
Full-Time Playing Career:
SHEFFIELD UNITED, signed January 1959
ALDERSHOT, signed July 1961
HALIFAX TOWN, signed July 1965
LINCOLN CITY, signed March 1968
BOSTON UNITED, signed June 1969
COLCHESTER UNITED, signed November 1972

Position: Wing-half
League Appearances: 247
League Goals: 8

Managerial Career:
BOSTON UNITED, June 1969 to November 1972
COLCHESTER UNITED, November 1972 to June 1975
BLACKBURN ROVERS, June 1975 to March 1978
BIRMINGHAM CITY, March 1978 to February 1982
OXFORD UNITED, March 1982 to June 1985
QUEEN'S PARK RANGERS, June 1985 to December 1988
NEWCASTLE UNITED, December 1988

Promotion:
1973–74 COLCHESTER UNITED from Division Four to
  Division Three
1979–80 BIRMINGHAM CITY from Division Two to
  Division One

1983–84 OXFORD UNITED from Division Three to
  Division Two
1984–85 OXFORD UNITED from Division Two to
  Division One

Relegation:

1978–79 BIRMINGHAM CITY from Division One to
  Division Two
1988–89 NEWCASTLE UNITED from Division One to
  Division Two

Honours:

Third Division Championship 1983–84 with Oxford United
Second Division Championship 1984–85 with Oxford United
Milk Cup Finalist 1985–86 with Queen's Park Rangers